Mindfulness

Made Easy

D1421045

❖ **Also in the *Made Easy* series** ❖

Mindfulness

Made Easy

Learn How to be Present and Kind –
to Yourself and Others

Ed Halliwell

HAY HOUSE

Carlsbad, California • New York City
London • Sydney • New Delhi

First published and distributed in the United Kingdom by:
Hay House UK Ltd, Astley House, 33 Notting Hill Gate, London W11 3JQ
Tel: +44 (0)20 3675 2450; Fax: +44 (0)20 3675 2451
www.hayhouse.co.uk

Published and distributed in the United States of America by:
Hay House Inc., PO Box 5100, Carlsbad, CA 92018-5100
Tel: (1) 760 431 7695 or (800) 654 5126
Fax: (1) 760 431 6948 or (800) 650 5115
www.hayhouse.com

Published and distributed in Australia by:
Hay House Australia Ltd, 18/36 Ralph St, Alexandria NSW 2015
Tel: (61) 2 9669 4299; Fax: (61) 2 9669 4144
www.hayhouse.com.au

Published and distributed in India by:
Hay House Publishers India, Muskaan Complex, Plot No.3, B-2,
Vasant Kunj, New Delhi 110 070
Tel: (91) 11 4176 1620; Fax: (91) 11 4176 1630
www.hayhouse.co.in

This book was previously published as *Mindfulness (Hay House Basics series)*,
ISBN: 978-1-78180-264-9

A catalogue record for this book is available from the British Library.

Trade paperback ISBN: 978-1-78817-265-3
Ebook ISBN: 978-1-78817-281-3

Interior illustrations © 123RF.com

Printed and bound in Great Britain by CPI Group (UK) Ltd, Croydon CR0 4YY

'If you know the point of balance,
You can settle the details.
If you can settle the details,
You can stop running around.
Your mind will become calm.
If your mind becomes calm,
You can think in front of a tiger.
If you can think in front of a tiger,
You will surely succeed.'

MENCIUS

Contents

PART IV: CHOICE

Mindfulness Practices

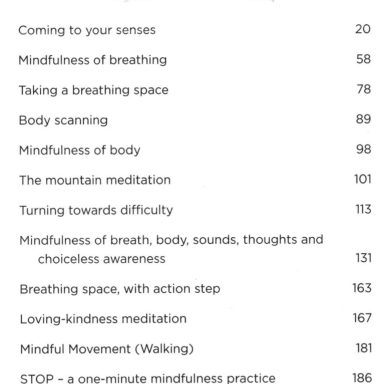

Introduction

In my mid-twenties, I became very stuck. I was working frantically and living hedonistically, trying to numb a nagging sense of doubt that the career and lifestyle I'd chosen were at odds with my values and aspirations. I sought happiness by chasing after pleasure and status, but the more I strived for contentment, the more it seemed out of reach. When yet another relationship fell apart, I did too, sinking into a deep and anxious depression.

Looking back now, I see my main trouble was I didn't know how to live well. I had very little understanding of how happiness *happens* – not just in terms of the activities that lead to wellbeing, but in how to work skilfully with experience itself. I had very little awareness of the patterns of thinking, feeling, relating and doing in which I was trapped, and so even when I recognized that something was wrong, I didn't really know what it was, or what to do about it. In desperation, I tried many fixes, but none seemed to help.

Actually, trying to get rid of my misery seemed to make it worse. Having spent years striving and running after pleasure, I was now trying to fight and run away from pain.

As a wellbeing strategy, it was just as flawed. I kept going round and round, faster and faster, like a dog chasing its tail.

After a lot of flailing around, it was suggested I learn to meditate. This was a turning point. Learning to be still and look inwards, I began to discover awareness, becoming familiar with patterns of mind and body that had unconsciously driven my behaviour. With practice, I learned it was possible – gradually and gently – to let go of being controlled by these patterns, and to develop a different way of being. A little space began to emerge, along with some relief. With this came the possibility of making new choices: ones guided by a sense of heart's calling, which at last I could listen to. I'd begun to discover mindfulness.

Around a dozen years after this turning point, my life feels quite different. I've long since left my old job, and now teach mindfulness to others. I was fortunate enough to find a partner, having learned something of what makes relationships work. From a place of despair, isolation and disconnection – of not knowing what to do or how to do it – I've been granted a measure of peace that previously looked unlikely.

This seems to have come not so much from chasing after dreams but from turning towards realities, getting to know them intimately, even when they're painful. It's come from cultivating a new approach to living. I didn't set out for this particular change to happen – it's appeared as a by-product of practice over time. It's an ongoing work-in-progress, a training that I now trust and delight in, even when it's not easy.

What does living well mean? Answers might come from two more questions: what is happening and how can we learn from it? If we're unaware of what's going on – not just at the surface of things, but in depth – then it's difficult for us to know what drives us, and for things to change. We may find ourselves in activity, but ignorant of the processes that lead us to act, we're doomed to repeat our habits. Unwittingly caught in our grooves, we're sleepwalking (or more likely sleep-running) through life.

When we start to pay attention to experience, with mindfulness, we can also begin to reflect on it. Not just by thinking, which often occurs on autopilot, but from a place of embodied understanding, an awareness of the world in and around us. This awareness can sense more deeply and spaciously the content of our lives, and also the ways we relate to it.

As we train in working with this deeper understanding, rather than being impelled into automatic reactions, the possibility of change arises. New perspectives can come, and we can explore new behaviour. Noticing what leads to wellbeing, and what doesn't, we can experiment with different choices. Attuning to the feedback we receive from our minds and bodies, we develop a connection with the world that can guide us through it more wisely.

This isn't esoteric. We can train the capacity for embodied awareness, through mindfulness practices that help us discover how to be and what to do. These ways have been known, employed and refined for thousands of years, and they're the subject of widespread current interest because scientific research is demonstrating many of their benefits, and because the world is in need of practical ways to wisdom. The intention of this book is to introduce you to some of these practices, as well as exploring attitudes that can be usefully brought to them. I hope you will find them as beneficial as I have.

How to Use This Book

The book is organized as a week-by-week training manual, with each of the nine chapters exploring aspects of mindfulness. They include key practices, an overview of the scientific findings that point to the benefits of mindfulness, and case studies that follow the experiences of four people who've learned to practise in recent years.

You can try reading one chapter per week, experimenting with the practices described in each – but it's also fine to dip in and out, or stay with one or two practices until you feel ready to continue. Mindfulness is not a linear process, and it's good to return to the basics and work with them over and over.

It can be very helpful to have an audio guide for mindfulness meditation, especially in the beginning, and I've recorded guided versions of all the practices in this book, available to download (or order on CD) at www.edhalliwell.com.

It's best not to be in a rush to 'get' mindfulness, as mindfulness can't be got by rushing, so please take your time. As we'll see, this is one training where you're encouraged not to focus on striving for results.

A word of caution

Sometimes, it isn't the right time to practise meditation intensively. When we're currently experiencing very strong feelings, moving into those feelings can feel overwhelming, especially if we're not used to it.

This can occur, for example, when we're very depressed, recently bereaved, heavily addicted, or going through some major transition in our lives. In these cases, it may make sense to wait a while – to make sure you have suitable support, and to train less intensively to begin with. It's a bit like wanting to run a marathon after breaking a leg: you'd need to allow some healing to take place before you start an exercise regime.

If you're in any doubt, or you feel overwhelmed when you practise, it may be worth consulting with an experienced mindfulness teacher or other health professional, to discuss the best way for you. This doesn't mean you're not a good candidate for training – just that the most mindful way for now might be to wait, or to work towards creating suitable conditions.

Part I

LAYING FOUNDATIONS

'In our world, everybody thinks of changing humanity, and nobody thinks of changing himself.'
Leo Tolstoy

Chapter 1

The Medicine of Mindfulness

'To live is the rarest thing in the world.
Most people exist, that is all.'
OSCAR WILDE

Mindfulness brings us to our senses, enabling us to live in and with reality. As we practise opening to the senses, a new way of being can emerge within us. We develop a friendly awareness of what's going on, and are able to learn from it.

Walking down the street, you hear the sound of a horse's hooves from behind. You turn to see a friend on top of the horse, which is galloping by at a furious pace. You call after the friend: 'Where are you going?' The rider yells back: 'I don't know. Ask the horse!'

Many of us live our lives like the friend in this scene: hurtling through the days, feeling driven, rather than in charge. Life may be happening, but are we really choosing our course? And when we *are* making choices, to what extent are they wise ones, expressing our true intent?

The cost of relentless *doing*

Surveys suggest that despite huge economic growth, people in Britain and the US are generally no happier than they were 50 years ago.[1] We may even be *less* happy than former generations: the World Health Organization warns that by 2030 depression will create the largest burden of any illness,[2] overtaking cancer, heart disease and diabetes.

We may be richer in monetary terms, but most of us agree that 'the pace of life and the number of things we have to do and worry about is a major cause of stress, unhappiness and illness'.[3] The pressure we feel to compete and achieve, pushing harder and faster and for longer hours, doesn't seem to lead to wellbeing, even if it produces material gains. Nevertheless, like the rider on the horse, we keep being driven,˙ perhaps without considering where we're headed, or why we might be going in that direction.

With all our modern means of communication, consumption of information has increased by 350 per cent over the last three decades.[4] Multi-tasking is often tried as a way to cope – if we can manage more things at once, perhaps we'll clear the decks? But research suggests this doesn't help; in fact, trying to multi-task reduces our productivity by as much as 40 per cent.[5] We waste energy by switching our attention from one thing to the next in quick succession. As T.S. Eliot put it, well before the creation of the internet, we get 'distracted from distraction by distraction'.

As we become more stressed, our mental capacity decreases – we feel overwhelmed and can't think straight. We're relegated to paying 'continuous partial attention'[6] – a fractured, frantic way of life that only frazzles us further.

Stress appears to shrink parts of the brain that help regulate mind and body functions, putting us at a greater risk of mental and physical illness.[7] In trying to get everywhere faster, we actually make our journey harder, and less enjoyable.

People are creatures of habit, and relentless doing (or thinking about doing) seems to have become an ingrained human tendency. Evolutionary biologists tell us this habit stems from benign intent – to survive and prosper, our ancestors learned to look ahead, be alert and responsive to possible threats, and to think back and learn from mistakes.

But when it gets out of hand, or is applied to situations in which we have little control, this 'doing' mode, as it's sometimes called, leads to anxiety and rumination. We can get so focused on solving problems that we miss the good we have right now. Dissatisfaction becomes our default condition.

Root causes of stress

Around 2,500 years ago, a great psychologist not only recognized this issue but saw its causes and worked out a remedy. By observing patterns of mind, body and behaviour, he realized that at the root of human distress is a tendency to cling, crave and resist. Each time we grasp at something, discomfort is inevitable. We also suffer when we reject our experience, wanting something other than what's actually happening. When we try to prevent what's already here, or hold on to what's changing, we engage in a losing battle.

Fortunately, said the psychologist, we get caught in these tendencies only due to lack of awareness. We play out our patterns in a state of semi-sleep, propelled through life by habits that have built up over time. The good news is we can begin to free ourselves from these habits – by becoming willing and able to look at our predicament, learning gently to let go of unhelpful old ways, and starting to engage with the world in a more conscious, courageous, and compassionate manner.

Such a transformation can occur by practising mindfulness. This means learning a set of skills that brings us to our senses, enabling us to live more in tune with present-moment reality. Using his own experience as a guide, the psychologist reported that mindfulness was 'all-helpful',[8] leading to real happiness.

The mindful path to wellbeing, he said, helps us arise from slumber. With this observation, the psychologist made his name. He became known as 'Buddha' – which means 'one who is awake'.

Mindfulness as medicine

Buddhism can seem like a religion, but it may be more helpful to see the basic message as medicine. We can taste and test mindfulness for ourselves. If we're able and willing to practise, we *can* find greater contentment. The path laid out is an applied training in the art of living well.

Over the centuries, many people have tried some or all of it, whether practising in the Buddhist tradition, through engaging with other contemplative paths, or by discovering similar insights and methods through their own ingenuity and investigation. They often report that, over time, the approach transforms their lives. It doesn't require belief – intrigued by his radiance, the Buddha's contemporaries reportedly asked him if he was a god: 'No,' he is said to have replied, 'I am awake.'

In modern times, analyses of the human condition have been gloomy. When describing his new science of psychoanalysis, Sigmund Freud said its aim was to turn neurotic misery into common unhappiness, while Western medicine has tended to focus on fixing broken body parts, until no more repair is feasible. So-called mental health problems, not easily treated with these methods, have often been swept under the carpet, or left to fester. The possibility of turning discontent into joy is an idea that's received scant attention.

But things are shifting. Scientific research and technology have become more sophisticated, and we now know the brain can change in ways once thought unlikely. Just as the body's muscles can be strengthened by exercise, areas of the brain can be activated, connected, and grown with training in certain skills.

We have long known that physical exercise has health-promoting benefits. Science is now showing that mindfulness – traditionally cultivated through meditation practice – is also good for us. These practices, it seems, have powerful effects on the brain and body that lead towards peace.

In the field of wellbeing, results from mindfulness research may be among the most interesting discoveries since it was found that physical exercise has health-promoting benefits. Non-religious mindfulness trainings have become more available, and many health practitioners have embraced them with interest.

Contentment, it turns out, isn't a lost cause. We know this intuitively: when asked, 86 per cent of people agreed that 'people would be much happier and healthier if they knew how to slow down and live in the moment'.[9]

Mindfulness: the science

Hundreds of mindfulness studies are published every year. The research has found that not only are mindful people more prone to wellbeing, but mindfulness training helps cultivate it. Below is a summary of what's been learned.

Overall health

A 2012 review looked at 31 high-quality trials of an eight-week mindfulness course (mindfulness-based stress reduction), and found it effective for working with anxiety, depression, stress and distress, as well as aspects of personal development such as ability to empathize and cope with life's challenges. Mindfulness was also found to be helpful for physical health.[1]

In 2013, a review with an even larger scope looked at 209 studies of mindfulness courses with a total of more than 12,000 participants, and concluded that mindfulness is 'an effective treatment for a variety of psychological problems, and is especially effective for reducing anxiety, depression, and stress'.[2]

Stress

Studies indicate that people who practise mindfulness experience less stress, and also have lower levels of the stress hormone cortisol.[3]

Depression

Combined data from six high-quality trials of another eight-week mindfulness course (mindfulness-based cognitive therapy) found it leads to an average 44 per cent reduction in relapse rates among people prone to depression. People who take the course also become kinder to themselves.[4]

Pain

After practising mindfulness meditation for 20 minutes a day over three days, people given a painful heat stimulus reported their pain as 40 per cent less intense and 57 per cent less unpleasant than before the training. They also showed less activity in the somatosensory cortex, an area of the brain associated with pain processing, and increased activity in areas of the brain involved in cognitive and emotional control.[5] Other studies have also reported significant effects of mindfulness on pain intensity.[6]

The immune system

Participants in an eight-week mindfulness programme were compared with another group following an eight-week exercise regime, and a third set of people who neither exercised nor meditated. They were all monitored to see who fell ill over the next cold and flu season.

The mindfulness group had half as many sick days as those who exercised, were ill for less time, and reported less severe symptoms. The group who did nothing fared worst of all.[7] Other studies have shown the benefits of mindfulness for speed of healing and the ability to cope with a wide variety of illnesses, including cancer, heart disease and diabetes.[8]

Cognitive skills

Mindfulness appears to have benefits for focus, concentration and memory.[9] Some studies suggest that it may aid creative, flexible problem-solving,[10] and people who practise meditation have been shown to make more rational decisions.[11]

Behaviour regulation

Mindfulness seems to help people manage addictive patterns with food, cigarettes and alcohol, as well as emotions and urges more generally.[12] People who practise mindfulness also tend to sleep better,[13] and engage in more pro-social and environmentally friendly actions.[14]

Relationships

Mindfulness helps us relate to others more skilfully. As well as cultivating empathy, which can lead to mutual understanding, mindful people feel more connected with others, are more likely to enjoy satisfying relationships, and are better able to cope with relationship conflicts.[15, 16]

Other studies

Taking a mindfulness course has been shown to reduce anger, rumination and medical symptoms, and improve people's sense of internal cohesion. Those who are more mindful tend to be more conscientious, independent, competent, resilient and optimistic, and less neurotic, absent-minded, reactive, and defensive.[17]

How does mindfulness happen?

It *is* possible to move towards wellbeing, but it doesn't occur in the way we might expect – through straining, searching and struggling for answers. Actually, the benefits seem to come from not doing much at all, at least to begin with, Rather, mindfulness means observing and feeling what's really going on in the moment.

To return to the story of the rider on the horse, practising mindfulness means that, instead of unconsciously digging in the heels and spooking the horse to go faster, our rider friend might begin to notice the feet clenching in fear – gripping on for dear life. They might become aware of a pulling back on the reins that strains the horse's neck.

Mindfulness means an open-hearted awareness of what's happening, and learning from what we find. This comes first of all from paying attention to the senses. Rather than getting caught up in ideas, we tune in to our world with awareness of sight, sound, feeling, taste and smell.

As we experience more fully this amazing sensory palette, we notice how thoughts occur as well as sensation, and we notice how this additional layer of concept often drives us, even though it isn't always an accurate reflection of events. We begin to realize that although we rarely question its validity, our thinking is often off-base, tricking us out of step with the truth.

We observe how our misinterpretations create stress – a tension between how things are and how we mistakenly perceive them to be, or would like them to be. This stress drives automatic thoughts which spin round and round, reigniting distressing sensations and leading to even more thoughts – a vicious cycle which keeps on pulling us into reaction and distraction.

Watching our own mind and body like our friend on their mount, we see how the horse bolts and feel how the rider panics. By noticing this, rather than getting caught up with it or struggling against it, we're already loosening the ties that bind. With gentleness, we bring our attention back to direct experience in the moment. We sit steady and lighten our grip.

Over time, as we practise opening and re-opening to sensory awareness – coming back to attention as the mind wanders – a different way of being (a real *wellbeing*) can unfold within us. By repeatedly shifting how we attend to experience, we strengthen the muscle of mindfulness.

Mindfulness and neuroplasticity

Neuroscience has shown that the brain changes with experience. For example, taxi drivers who have ferried passengers around London for years have larger hippocampi, a region of the brain important for spatial awareness and memory, compared to newer cab drivers. It appears the practice of taxi driving grows this part of the brain over time.[1]

Similarly, experienced musicians show higher grey matter volume in motor, auditory and visual-spatial regions,[2] suggesting their brains have been altered through hours of daily practice. When the brain is damaged – such as during a stroke – it is possible to recover lost capacity through rehabilitation therapy. Other areas of the brain take over from those damaged by the stroke.[3]

The brain's ability to change and adapt in response to experience is known as neuroplasticity. Just as how we exercise affects the body's weight, health, flexibility and strength, the same is true of the brain. This process can happen quite quickly: learning to juggle or play the piano over just a few days alters brain density.[4] Remarkably, even mentally rehearsing piano keystrokes results in similar brain changes, almost as if you were actually playing.

This is empowering news because it suggests that we aren't stuck with our old brains and our old habits. We can plough new furrows, cultivating freedom to shape the future, based on what we do in the present, or how we train the mind.

Researchers have explored the neuroplastic changes that occur with mindfulness training, and are finding that practitioners' brains seem to reflect their expertise. Activity, structure and volume are different in parts of the pre-frontal cortex,[5] the most recently evolved area of the brain, which is associated strongly with reasoning and decision-making. Experienced meditators also show high levels of gamma wave activity, which is thought to be related to increased awareness.[6]

Changes start to be seen in the brains of new meditators after a few days or weeks of training. As they practise mindfulness, regions of the brain related to learning, memory, mind-body awareness, cognitive control, emotional reactivity, sense of self and other markers of wellbeing are all affected.[7]

It doesn't take much, it appears, for patterns of activity and connectivity in the brain to shift. As new grooves are formed in our ways of seeing, relating and behaving, so these are reflected and perhaps reinforced by neural shifts.

Gentleness and commitment

Like any other skill, mindfulness takes a kind of effort. We're learning a new way of being with our minds, bodies and environment, and this may bring up feelings of awkwardness, discomfort, disappointment or irritation. We may fall off the horse sometimes, and think we'll never get back on. We might sometimes believe that mindfulness isn't for us, or that we're a hopeless case.

Some descriptions of mindfulness training suggest it's more like riding an elephant than a horse, which perhaps gives an indication of the challenge (and fun) that may lie ahead. But with guidance and a gentle commitment, we can work with the impulsive reactions that govern us, perhaps even finding that, like a tamed wild animal, they might eventually become our friends and helpers.

Practice: Coming to your senses

Mindfulness begins when we move from a mode of doing and thinking, and into a way of being, where sensing takes centre stage. Because most of us aren't used to working with our senses in this way, it helps to practise. For this five senses practice, the only equipment you need is yourself, a chair, and a glass of water.

Allow about three minutes for each stage (15 minutes in total). Once you've read the guidance, put the book down while you practise, one sense at a time. For a guided audio version of this practice, and all the other practices in this book, please visit www.edhalliwell.com.

Feeling

If possible, sit upright (although not stiffly so) on the chair, with your back self-supporting and feet on the ground. Let your hands come to rest on the thighs, and, if you like, close your eyes.

What sensations do you notice? How are your feet feeling: perhaps there's contact between the soles of the feet and the socks, shoes or the floor? Can you feel the weight of your sit bones on the seat? How about in your back – what sensations are here? Do you feel air on your face? What temperature is it just now – warmer or cooler?

And what about internal sensations? Are you noticing any aching, itching, or buzzing? Or maybe there's not much sensation at the moment – a numbness, perhaps? Be aware of the location of any feeling (or lack of feeling), and whether it's changing in intensity. You don't have to try to hold on to or get rid of sensations, or even to name them. See if you can just allow them to be experienced.

Hearing

Now, as you let body sensations fade into the background, allow sounds to be noticed. What are you hearing? You don't have to go searching for sounds: wait for them to come to you, as if your ears were microphones, receiving and registering vibrations. Louder, softer, closer, further away, short or long sounds?

Or sudden, repeating and continuous sounds? Are they high or low pitch? Perhaps there's silence, or gaps in-between sounds – are you noticing these too? Open your microphone ears and let hearing come in, whether the sounds seem pleasant or unpleasant. Whatever symphony is playing right now, can you let it be heard?

Seeing

Now open the eyes to seeing. Rather than fixing on what you can see as 'things' (e.g. table, chair, book, carpet, etc.), see if you can let the visual field be colours, shapes, shades, or lines. Allow the eyes to linger rather than darting about. Be interested in depth and height and shade.

If you find yourself thinking about what you're seeing – drawn into a memory or a concern, or automatically giving things a name as they come into view – that's fine, just acknowledge that the mind has wandered into thought, and gently come back to seeing.

Smelling

Perhaps closing the eyes again, allow yourself to smell. Whether what you're smelling seems nice or not so nice, let there be a connection with the odours. Is there more than one fragrance, and if so, how are they mixed together? If there are no smells, what's the smell of 'no smell'? The in-breaths don't need to be deep – see if you can let breath happen naturally and offer curiosity to the coming and going of smell sensation. Isn't it amazing to have a nose?

Tasting

Pick up the glass of water, and take a sip. Notice the arising of sensation on the tongue as the liquid makes contact. How does it taste? Clear, cool, refreshing? Let the describing words fade into the distance, allowing the sensation of taste itself be known.

Gently swirl the water around your mouth, and notice if the flavour changes – perhaps as it mixes with saliva. Does it become warmer, duller, thicker? Let these sensations be experienced. Decide when you're ready to swallow the water; notice the dissolving of taste – does any trace remain, and if so, for how long? Now take another, maybe bigger, sip and repeat – are the sensations the same, or do they seem different? What, if anything, has changed?

When you've practised working with each of the senses, you might reflect on any differences between this way of sensing and how you normally relate with your environment. If it seems different, how so? What were you doing that made it this way? Be interested in the answers that come up. Is the quality of your experience changed by how you attend to it?

Week 1: practices to explore

- Work with the Coming to your senses practice once a day. If you like, explore different locations for practising, noticing what happens each time. For tasting, you can use any food or drink.

- Choose one daily activity that you normally do on autopilot (e.g. brushing your teeth, walking the dog, washing the dishes, etc.) and practise bringing mindfulness to it each day this week, experiencing it with the senses. Notice what happens.

* Bring awareness to the senses at other times, whenever you remember. When you find yourself caught in rumination or distraction, gently bring yourself back to sensing. What effect does this have, if any?

* Ask yourself: what are my intentions for exploring mindfulness? What would I like to learn? If you like, write these down, noticing how it feels to put them on paper, and what it's like to look at them written in front of you.

* Once you've recorded your intentions, see if you can let go of any explicit attempt to achieve them. Can you allow intentions to inspire your exploration, but without making them a goal to measure yourself against? Can you allow yourself just to let go into mindfulness training – giving it your full energy as you focus on what's happening right now?

Simon's experience

I'd just turned 50 and thought being happy would arrive at some point if I kept trying hard enough. It was August, which is always when my work goes quiet, and once again I'd built this up to be the time when life would be wonderful. And it wasn't.

That August my mum wasn't very happy and I'd scraped my car. There were all these hassles happening in my perfect month! They weren't particularly serious, but they didn't fit my picture. I was doing what I'd always done

– trying to reach contentment by working very hard for most of the year and then having a huge expectation that time off was going to be great. When those expectations weren't met, the frustration was enormous.

I got to a breaking point where I realized my aspirations and what I was doing to achieve them weren't meeting – one wasn't leading to the other. It took almost a mini-breakdown for me to look for something different. I saw that if I carried on like that it wasn't going to lead to my holy grail of happiness.

Soon after my birthday I started reading a book that had been recommended to me by a friend – it was based on the Mindfulness-Based Stress Reduction course. I found it really useful for exploring new perspectives on things. Just at that time my partner said she was going on a mindfulness course, and we realized that it was the course of the book I was reading. I joined her on the course and it was like practising what I'd read. The book opened the door and the course enabled me to walk through it.

Ann's experience

The trigger of my eldest son leaving home made me realize family life was never going to be the same, and it led to quite a severe depression. I just felt unbalanced, and it was also the start of a difficult menopause. Once I felt a bit better, my GP said I needed to have some strategies for coping with the underlying anxieties, so I had some counselling, and I also booked a mindfulness course.

*One of my biggest problems was that I didn't control
my own life. I let others control me to the point where
I didn't have my own identity. I felt that I always had to
please other people, doing things I didn't want to, and I
realized that was a source of my anxiety. When I made
decisions I wasn't making them in an informed way – I
was like a hamster on a treadmill, just going from one
thing to another without having time to breathe.*

Andy's experience

*I was introduced to meditation in the early 1990s, by
a friend who was interested in Buddhism. We were
backpacking around India and he went off to a retreat.
He'd split up from his partner and was really struggling,
but there was a different depth to him when he came
out. I was interested, but I was also a little cynical.*

*In my late twenties/early thirties, I had a 'break-up', as
I call it, I was drinking too much, travelling all over the
world with my job. It was unsustainable, living life at
that speed, and I ended up in quite a bad place. I was
in hospital for a period of time because I'd lost touch
with reality.*

*I recovered from that, but I still carried a lot of anxiety.
I'd get very anxious in public places. I was also beating
myself up about stuff from the past – each day I'd have
dozens of what I call 'shame attacks'. Thoughts about
the past were blocking my ability to be present.*

*The opportunity to do a mindfulness course came up
through work. A lot of people said it would be good for
me if I could slow down and be less busy in my mind.*

Catherine's experience

I knew I had a good life, but I didn't seem able to appreciate it. As a mum, I was constantly living in the future, a few minutes, a few hours, or a few days ahead, striving hard to make things right. Life was going by and I was in 'management mode'.

With my kids, I tended to think I had to sort out every problem right away or they would never succeed in the future. Wanting to be in control and wanting everything to be perfect piled on a load of expectations. There was a feeling that if I didn't do parenting right, it'd have consequences down the road, which meant I felt threatened and under pressure.

I'd been aware of mindfulness and meditation, but I didn't think it was for me because I had too much to do. I thought I wouldn't be able to sit down for a long time. I also thought it might be a bit shallow, more of a relaxation technique that would benefit me in the immediate term – maybe like exercising and getting the endorphins. I didn't understand then that it was a practice, and that you can train your brain to think differently. But mindfulness kept coming up in the reading I was doing, and with the people I spoke to, so I thought: I've got to give it a go, with an open mind, to see if it works.

SUMMARY

- Mindfulness is a powerful practice of mind and body that can move us in the direction of peace.

- For this we need to pay attention with the senses, which connect us to what's actually happening right now.

- More mindful people are prone to optimal wellbeing, and training in mindfulness helps people cultivate greater happiness, in mind, body and behaviour.

- Neuroscience has shown that the brain changes with experience. Practising mindfulness changes the brain in ways that are associated with wellbeing.

- Mindfulness begins when we move from a mode dominated by doing and thinking, and into a way of being, in which sensing takes centre stage. We can use the Coming to your senses practice to help cultivate this.

Chapter 2

Planting Seeds

*'No one can help you, not even your
most loving mother and father, as much
as your own mind, well trained.'*
THE BUDDHA

*Wellbeing seems to come as much from the approach we
bring to experience – from how we choose to see it and
work with it – as from what's actually happening and what
we decide to do. If we can cultivate healthy approaches
to experience, we'll probably feel better, no matter what's
going on.*

Ten Cs of mindfulness

Certain attitudes are helpful as we enter into mindfulness
training. This chapter outlines 10 ways of approaching life
that you might like to cultivate as part of your practice.
Some of these attitudes may feel no more than seeds in
your being right now, but just as seeds can flower when
tended, so attitudes can grow if we nurture them. All the
seeds in this chapter begin with the letter C.

Commitment

There's a cartoon that shows a new meditator, with a bubble of worries rising from her head. The caption reads: 'I know I've only been practising for two minutes, but meditation isn't bringing me the peace of mind I was promised.'

It's important to understand that mindfulness isn't a quick fix – like any skill, it takes time to learn, and its rewards don't always come immediately. When we slow down and look at our minds and bodies, we might not like everything we find. We may notice pain, anxiety or desperate thoughts. We might find impatience, anger, doubt, or sadness.

Maybe the urge to give up will arise, or an idea that we should feel better, happier, more peaceful. We might decide we're not suited to mindfulness. Over time, we learn that whatever comes up is workable, but unless we make a steady commitment, we risk losing heart at an early stage, before the practice has time to bear fruit. Unlearning old habits and developing new ones takes patient effort. It helps to meditate each day, whether the weather of our mind is bright or gloomy.

Suggestion Look at your schedule – is there some space and time you can devote to mindfulness practice? Can you designate a place in your home where you can be uninterrupted for two, five, 10 or more minutes a day? Can you prepare this space and protect it from the demands of people, phones and computers, just for this period of time?

Compassion

When it comes to learning or making changes, many of us have been told – or perhaps tell ourselves – that we 'need to work harder', 'haven't got it in us' or 'should be doing better'. Our internal slave-driver barks orders, and we often react by striving harder for perfection, or refusing to engage at all. It's all too easy to make 'not being mindful' another stick to be beaten with, and aim to compensate by straining for success, berating ourselves or feeling guilty.

Mindfulness is a training where being critical and trying too hard doesn't produce results – mindfulness isn't mindfulness without gentleness. So, compassion is key. Whenever we hear the voice of the slave-driver, telling us we're not doing it right, or that we're a useless meditator, we can use this as a reminder to open up to kindness. This work is a gardening of the heart, and you can't grow a flower by screaming at it.

We can notice when we're hard on ourselves (and others), gently recognizing harsh judgements for what they are. In this way, we create a loving space to learn. Perhaps we can bring compassion to the slave-driver in us, even as we decide not to follow orders.

Suggestion Listen to your internal voice – is there a running commentary playing in your head? How does this voice speak to you? Does it cajole and criticize, or is it kind and caring? Is this *your* voice, or does it come from someone or somewhere else – maybe a parent, a teacher, or the television? How do you normally relate to this voice – do you believe it, reject it, or not even know it's there?

Experiment first with just noticing the voice – a bit like you'd notice the chatter on a radio in the background. If it's a slave-driver, notice how it feels to be constantly shaming, getting angry, or belittling. Experiment with offering the voice a compassionate space. You might say: 'It must be difficult to always be on the attack. I'm not going to believe what you say, but perhaps you'd like a hug?'

Curiosity

A scholarly student visited his teacher's home for tea. An avid reader, the student had formed many opinions about what there was to learn. As the student talked, the teacher filled his tea cup to the brim, and kept on pouring as it overflowed. The student protested, and the teacher explained: 'This cup is like your mind – there isn't any space. If you want to study with me, first you must empty your cup.'

Like the student, we may cram our minds with ideas. Intellectual knowledge can be good, but when we become stuffed with concepts, this can get in the way. Curiosity means we're prepared to rest in not-knowing. Instead of meeting the world with expectation, we move towards it in a spirit of interest, with an open mind and heart.

We let go of reassuring attempts to confirm what we already think, and instead offer a friendly engagement with what's actually here. We can look, listen, smell, taste and feel, not limiting our view by laying old maps onto fresh terrain. We allow ourselves to explore the world, re-discovering in every moment if it fits with preconception.

Suggestion Open up to what's sometimes called 'beginner's mind': a willingness to park prior learning and experience the world afresh. We don't have to give up being smart – real wisdom offers space for new perspectives.

Courage

The mindfulness road can be rocky. It's brave to stay with the present moment, especially when we don't like what's happening. This courage is known as an 'approach' mentality. Approach-minded people move towards challenge with interest. They don't just push away or run from difficulties. When driving in the snow, it's better to turn into a skid, even though it runs against instinct. Sometimes, the skids in life are the same.

The opposite of approach is avoidance, which is a sign of poor psychological health. Avoidance means habitually fleeing from fears: turning away from the skids. Of course, it's good to stay out of danger when we can – it doesn't make sense to put our hand in a fire – but when avoidance becomes a default setting, an automatic response to everything unpleasant, we restrict our range of responses.

In avoidant mode, we might never go to unfamiliar places, try new things, or explore possibilities that don't fit our existing schema. Life might feel safer, but also small and restricted. When we run or hide from anything painful, we don't practise meeting challenges wisely. When troubling things find us, as they usually do, we're unlikely to be ready. We're easily overwhelmed.

If an event, sensation or thought is present, no amount of struggling will make it *not* be here, *in this moment*. There may be things we can do to change the future, but only by meeting and working with what's going on right now. Curious though it may seem at first, by gently embracing pain, sadness, anger, loss, fear, or whatever is bothering us, we can develop a resilience that helps us live fully.

Suggestion The way we hold our bodies affects our experience.[1] To cultivate courage, we can take a dignified posture. Sometimes, people think courage means tensing up and getting ready to fight, but that's not what's meant here. Real courage is a willingness to be touched by life – to connect and co-operate with things as they are.

When sitting, standing or moving, feel your feet making connection with the Earth – this is an embodiment of groundedness. Feel your body rising up to the sky. Feel your chest open, its movements in tune with the rhythm of your breath. Let your shoulders drop, and the head and neck be balanced. Feel your beating heart at the core of your being. You don't have to force it – gently experiment with this way of being, and notice what happens.

Centring

Where is your mind? Ask most Westerners and chances are they'll point to their heads. To many of us, mindfulness suggests a cognitive quality, something to do with thinking and the brain. But this is only part of the story. We don't just exist from the neck up; we are also bodies, and by recognizing and attending to physical sensations, we can connect to fields of intuition.

In the story of the rider and the horse, which do you most identify with, the rider or the horse? Many people think they're the rider, trying to control a wayward beast. Actually, though, we are rider *and* horse, which represent qualities of mind and body. And the horse isn't wayward – it just isn't being handled with care. In fact, the horse is the rider's best friend – able to bear heavy loads and negotiate tricky terrain with nimbleness and skill. When danger approaches, it's often the horse that senses it first.

By opening our perception to and from the body, we can be aware of the wonder of physical form. We can appreciate the breath and blood and organs that keep us alive – as well as hearing and responding to the messages that come from body sensations. The body is the home of the senses, which offer us a window to direct experience. Centred from the body, we're in the saddle of life.

Suggestion Check in with your horse. What's happening in your body right now? Is there fatigue, energy, tension, relaxation, discomfort, restlessness, peace, or something else? Where do you notice these arising? Can you describe the sensations?

Co-operation

A wise teacher was once asked: 'What is the secret to your happiness?' The reply came back: 'A wholehearted co-operation with the unavoidable.' When the present moment is boring, irritating, frightening or painful, we may not *want* to co-operate. We may fear this will feel like resignation or self-betrayal, that we're failing to fight an unfair situation, or that we'll be overwhelmed.

We may not be able to change our situation, but we can always change ourselves. The word co-operate means 'to work with': and to work with our situation requires alignment. We can let go of the struggle for things to be different. We can stop trying to fix ourselves by battling: with pain, depression, anxiety, or whatever else ails us.

We can let go of chasing future pleasures in a way that blinds us to present-moment joy. Ceasing our striving to get somewhere else, we gently drop into feeling where we are. We can start to relax, even if what we're experiencing is uncomfortable. Releasing our tension, we're no longer in a state of war, with ourselves or the world. This is the 'co' of co-operation.

Aligned with the reality of circumstance, we may then be ready to 'operate', to begin to explore some activity. Continuing to check in with our senses, the action we take may be more harmonious. When we feel the tide shift in a different direction, we're able to readjust. We're starting to ride the waves of life with equanimity, going with the flow.

Suggestion Notice: are you tuned in with what's happening, or are you trying to fight or run from it, wishing you were somewhere else, or feeling something different? Let go of judging what you find: if you notice you're not in tune, can you let go of fighting or running from that realization too?

Connecting

By centring and co-operating, we enable connection to occur. Offering awareness to thoughts and sensations, we can experience their energies fully, touching in with courage and compassion. Feeling the pulses of life, we really are alive. We may be more open to pain, but perhaps less likely to suffer from it, and we get to feel the joy of pleasure more exquisitely too. If a sensation signals that something *is* harmful, we may be more attuned to the danger, and more able to respond appropriately.

In mindfulness training, we cultivate connection with our inner world – thoughts, sensations and impulse. We start to know and become friends with ourselves. With this internal attunement as our ground, we can also practise connecting with the places and people around us. Rather than refusing to look at what's going on, putting up the shutters to a seemingly hostile world, can we develop a flexible engagement that enables ebb and flow?

Suggestion Look for a community of practitioners with whom you can share the delights and challenges of mindfulness. Maybe there's a course, group or centre near you (see the further resources section for possibilities). Mindfulness doesn't work so well as a solo sport – as we get to know ourselves, it helps to connect with others.

Explore avenues of connection in the environment too – open your senses to trees, sky, grass, or air as you walk outside. You don't have to live somewhere stunning – are there aspects of your neighbourhood you haven't paid attention to? Buildings, pavements, parks or ponds?

Pay attention to internal spaces too, such as your home and work environment – do these have an influence on the inner space of your mind and body? Notice patterns of thought and sensation as you enter and leave different places, and meet different people. What are these telling you?

Confidence

Many millions of people have practised mindfulness over many, many centuries. Just because something has endured through the ages doesn't necessarily mean it's a good thing, but experienced practitioners often say they feel happier, kinder and lighter than when they began.

Scientific research points to the same thing: mindfulness brings more contentment, more compassion, more capacity to live well. When people who've undergone a physical training programme report improved health, or you're informed by your doctor that exercise is good for you, do you believe them? Could you allow yourself the same kind of confidence in mindfulness?

Confidence doesn't mean expectation, which tries to transport us to an imagined future. If you practise with the expectation of results (or if you're sceptical, the expectation of *no* results), you've already moved out of the moment and into a fantasy of what you think or hope might happen. Confidence here is meant more as a kind of trust, a willingness to use others' reports as fuel for the journey – giving us the impetus to stay on the road for ourselves. In time, once your practice has had a chance to flower, you can make your own assessment about whether mindfulness helps.

Suggestion Talk to others who have started practising. If you don't know anyone, and there's nowhere near you where people meet to train, look online for community resources. Sites like Everyday mindfulness (www.everyday-mindfulness.org) have forums where you can discuss your practice, while mindful.org offers a range of articles on the art, science and practice of mindfulness.

Cheerfulness

Cheerfulness means making joyous contact with life on its terms. It's not the same as crude positive thinking – trying to make things alright by thinking nice thoughts. If you find discontent within, you don't have to fabricate happiness. Being cheerful doesn't require you to try to be happy – it means opening your heart with appreciation.

Of course, you might say, it's easy to do this when life seems beautiful and things are going my way, but how can I be cheerful in the midst of sadness and anger, loss and illness, difficulty and disappointment? How can I have a sense of humour when I notice my rushing or resisting, my 'negative' thoughts, my pain – all the things I find frustrating?

It may seem a tall order, or even foolish, to be cheerful when things are unpleasant, but it seems that only by moving in this direction can we free ourselves from the stress that comes with challenge and change. Why compound a difficult experience with an attitude of misery? We may have no control over the experience, but we do have some with our attitude to it. In gently working to meet the difficult cheerfully, we hold a key to transformation.

Suggestion When problems arise, ask yourself: 'Could I open to this experience from a place of good cheer?' Notice what happens when you practise this. There is no need to pretend that events bringing sadness are suddenly ones to laugh about. We can still feel disappointment or anger, but could we practise cheerfulness at the same time?

Coming back

Most of us aren't constantly courageous, committed and centred. We don't always feel compassionate. Sometimes we experience doubt and separation, not confidence and connection. We get bored more than curious, and we don't feel like co-operating today. Cheerful? Forget it.

This is okay. We don't have to strive for perfection. We can allow ourselves to be who we are, where we are. Just *noticing* this is itself an act of co-operation, of compassion. It's more than good enough. The wonderful thing is, as soon as we've noticed what's happening, we're already back in mindfulness. When we see with eyes of awareness that we're bored, fearful, distracted, or depressed, we're no longer caught up in those things. This is worth celebrating.

However we're feeling, the very fact of knowing and being willing to experience it, makes the situation workable. We don't have to cajole, force or struggle our way back to awareness, or criticize ourselves for having wandered into unconsciousness – we can just notice. This process of noticing, again and again, is right at the heart of mindfulness practice.

Suggestion Bring awareness to patterns of distraction. Ask yourself at intervals: 'Am I here or elsewhere? Am I awake or unconscious?' Notice the effect of asking the question – does this return you to presence? If you find yourself forgetting to ask, set an alarm on your phone to ring a few times a day, or post reminders around your house. Make the reminders friendly rather than hectoring: 'Hello – are you at home right now?'

What mindfulness is not...

Misconceptions of mindfulness can hinder our practice. Letting go of beliefs such as the ones below can change the experience of meditation.

You're supposed to empty your mind

Many people give up meditating because they can't empty their mind of thoughts. But thinking isn't bad – it's okay to have thoughts, including in mindfulness practice. The invitation in most meditation practices is to let thoughts pass through the mind, neither following nor rejecting them. Striving to be rid of thoughts actually sets us up for a battle with the mind – thoughts tend not to go away on order. By dropping that goal, we're dropping a struggle that intensifies stress.

You're supposed to relax

Seeking calm moves us away from the moment, which may or may not feel calm. If we're tense, bored, angry, or sad, that *is* how we're feeling, and noticing and being with that is mindfulness. If we let go of resistance to what's here, relaxation may arise, even in the midst of unpleasant experience. But trying to grasp for the situation we'd like, rather than opening to the present that's here, is a recipe for tension.

It's doing nothing, and that can't help

Mindfulness practice may *look* like doing nothing, but by training ourselves to tune in to reality, we're engaging in important work. Most of us are in the stressful habit of seeking some other reality. To find relief, we need to stop trying so hard. Action may come, but we also need to learn when and how *not* to act.

It's a passive approach

If we're not resisting and battling, then aren't we giving up, being weak, failing to tackle the problems of the world? It's true there's a lot of stress around, and much of it is caused by unconscious action, patterns of habitual doing played out from habit. It takes courage and energy to tune in to life, and by moving into mindfulness, the stress of the world is eased as we learn to stop adding to it. With awareness, any action we take is more likely to bring relief.

It's navel-gazing self-centredness

Taking time for meditation, especially when there may be others depending on us, is sometimes considered selfish, an unaffordable luxury. Actually, mindfulness is even more important when we're under pressure, which may drive us to react impulsively and unskilfully. Far from being selfish, our training is key to caring for others well.

It's an escape from life

Sometimes, meditation is promised as a bypass to bliss – a way out of life's problems. But mindfulness means engaging with the now, which can sometimes be messy and difficult. Ironically, by trying to get to a place of easy enlightenment, we may be denying reality, which only makes this moment *more* difficult to handle. Mindfulness isn't an escape – it's a full, heartful engagement with the world.

Week 2: practices to explore

- This week, choose one of the Cs of mindfulness above, and practise noticing it in your own being. How does it already manifest in you? When and how is it expressed? Using the suggestions from this chapter as a guide, explore opening to this quality further, letting it arise and unfold within you. You don't have to try to get more of it or make it grow – your job is simply to take care of the seed, nurturing without expectation.

- Each week for the rest of the course, experiment with choosing another C to work with in the same way. It's also fine to stay with one for longer, or to come back to one you've already practised with. Listen to what feels right for you.

- Choose another daily activity that you normally do on autopilot (e.g. brushing your teeth, walking the dog, washing the dishes, etc.) and practise bringing mindfulness to it each day this week.

- Continue to work with the coming to your senses practice, once a day this week.

Simon's experience

Co-operation is a massive part of mindfulness. It's so easy to get frustrated with what you can't change, but you can always change one thing and that's your attitude. Our house looks out over a field, and there's a possibility that housing will be built there within the next five years. I don't want houses at the end of our garden, so what am I going to do? There are three possibilities: the building happens and we move house, the building happens and we stay where we are, or the building doesn't happen.

Actually, all these options are okay and that makes it a lot easier to deal with the process of trying to prevent the building from happening in a calm, mindful and non-reactive way. It enables acceptance of the outcome, even if I don't get what I want. Maybe we can move to somewhere even nicer and treat it as an opportunity?

Ann's experience

On the mindfulness course I took, a lot of us felt bad if we didn't do our practice. We beat ourselves up. But then I came to realize that part of being mindful is not having to berate yourself. If you don't practise for one day, the Earth isn't going to cave in. In some ways that gives you more space to practise because you're not putting that pressure on yourself. So then I started to apply that compassionate attitude to other things. I thought: Why am I putting pressure on myself and creating anxiety?

I do still get anxious, but I recognize it and then I know I've got something I can do about it. I can do a mindfulness practice or think: You've just fallen into a habit again – you don't have to get in a tizzy.

Andy's experience

I notice a deeper sense of connection when I practise mindfulness. It gives me a feeling of community, a connection to a wider world. I go to a regular practice group and we learn from each other. I've also been going to other mindfulness-related events and there are certain attitudes I see that I really respect, and which I'd like more of. I'm working towards it.

Catherine's experience

I can remember getting really annoyed during the first meditation we did on the course because I was uncomfortable. We talked in the group afterwards and I admitted this. The teacher said: 'It's okay, you're allowed to be irritated,' and I was like, 'Oh! Okay.'

It was really powerful because after that, every time I was irritated at home, with the kids or myself, I started saying: 'I'm annoyed, but that's okay; I'm allowed.' It's an amazing relief to be able to think like that, with compassion. It reduces the irritation because you're not fighting yourself as much, and you're not judging or blaming yourself for what you're feeling.

It's allowing yourself to be human, really – supporting yourself and being a good friend to yourself. Mindfulness has stopped me beating myself up so much.

SUMMARY

- Certain qualities are useful as we travel on the path of mindfulness. Just as seeds can flower when tended, so these qualities can grow as we nurture them.

- Ten Cs (seeds) of mindfulness are: Curiosity, Commitment, Courage, Compassion, Centring, Co-operation, Connection, Confidence, Cheerfulness and Coming Back.

- You don't have to try to get more of these qualities, or try to force them to grow in you – your job is to take care of the seed.

- There are some common misconceptions about what mindfulness is (such as emptying the mind or escaping from the world). Letting go of these can change our experience of meditation.

Part II

AWARENESS

'The only true voyage of discovery... would be not to visit strange lands but to possess other eyes.'

MARCEL PROUST

Chapter 3

Learning to Look

*'The faculty of voluntarily bringing back a
wandering attention, over and over again, is
the very root of judgement, character and
will... An education which should improve this
faculty would be an education par excellence.'*

WILLIAM JAMES

*How can we start to see more clearly? First, we need to
learn how to pay attention. Because the mind is so used
to wandering off, a good way to train is to practise placing
and re-placing it on an object such as the breath. Each time
we remember to return to the breath, with kindness, we're
strengthening our capacity to be more fully awake.*

The untamed human mind is sometimes likened to a
drunken monkey that's been bitten by a scorpion. In a
chaotic bid to run from its pain, the monkey leaps from
tree to tree, frantically seeking relief. It cannot be still, even
for a moment. Mental agitation happens mostly without
our conscious awareness. Until we choose to direct the
mind, and notice how difficult that can be, or find ourselves
hurtling on a train of unwanted thoughts (such as in the

distressing ruminations that often accompany anxiety and depression), we might not even notice the constant whirring. It's as if it's all happening on autopilot.

There are advantages to this autopilot. Mind and body mechanisms have evolved to deal with threats to survival, so when we're faced with an approaching fire or an assailant with a weapon, the autopilot reacts fast, either getting us out the way or preparing us for defence.[1] When our life is at risk, stopping to consider the options could be fatal, so it's good that our automatic reactions are quick and unreflective.

Living in the past

There *are* drawbacks, however. Thoughts occur in the mind unbidden, based as much on what's expected as what's *actually* happening. Working at speed, the autopilot takes mental shortcuts and makes guesses, unconsciously based on what's been learned before, rather than a full appreciation of the here and now.

This process makes use of what's called implicit memory,[2] in which previous experiences are unconsciously stored and brought to bear on actions in the present. This means we're partly seeing current situations with eyes of the past, simultaneously projecting into a possible future as we imagine likely dangers and rewards.

Let's say you were bitten by a dog when you were young. Now you're an adult, each time a friendly canine approaches, thoughts may appear, saying: *Danger! Don't go near! This animal could harm you!*, along with sensations of gut-churning, tight muscles and a rapid heartbeat. These thoughts and sensations – preparing you to fight or flee –

might save your life in times of real threat, but in this case they're based on a memory rather than present-moment risk. Once, when you were small and a dog seemed large, you got hurt. That was one dog, yet you're now running from (or tensing up at) all dogs.

Panic arises as a happily panting hound approaches, and you miss out on the joy of petting a friendly creature. Because your reaction happens on autopilot, you may never realize how or why it is skewed. Even if you understand intellectually that your behaviour is out of kilter, powerful thoughts and impulses may override any reasoning. Anxiety trumps logic. Dogs must be avoided. Fearful of what might happen again, you're living in the past, projecting into an imagined future.

While for some of us it might be dogs that frighten, for others it could be exams, or public speaking, or aeroplanes or spiders. Each in our own way, we learn from, and are limited by, past experience, particularly if our reactions are unconscious and in charge.

Negativity bias

Another issue is negativity bias.[3] The human mind and body has evolved to scan for danger, and it does so out of proportion to risk. This makes sense from a survival standpoint: if we space out on something hazardous – an oncoming car, say – that could be the end of the road for us. If, on the other hand, we miss a pleasant experience – a sunset, petting a dog, a friend's greeting – then from a survival point of view, it's no big shakes. Not having such experiences won't kill us.

Those of our ancestors who spotted serious survival threats, such as a predator in the bushes, were more likely to pass on their genes to offspring. Those who stopped to smell the flowers in the hedgerow (but didn't see the lurking animal therein) might have enjoyed a momentary pleasant sensation, but this could soon have turned to pain, and possibly extinction.

So we've evolved to tune in to the fearful more than the reassuring, to focus on problems rather than joys, with a bias to the unpleasant rather than the pleasant. Our mind is drawn to the possibility of risk, though most of the time there isn't an imminent threat. We see a rope, and our mind says it's a snake. We hear a rustle in the bushes and our mind says it's a murderer, not a mouse. Many of us find we're seduced by the news, which reminds us of and inclines us towards all the bad things that are happening in the world.

Our bias for the negative wires us for survival, but not for happiness – like news bulletins, we tend to give scant airtime to all the pleasant moments and supportive interactions that take place every day. On the basis of bitter experience, both over the course of human history and in our own lives, the autopilot mind acts from the perspective that there's no time for debate or ambiguity when we might be under threat. Using the example of being afraid of dogs after being bitten, it seems better to miss a hundred happy pups and a hundred pleasant pats than to risk repeating previous suffering, or worse.

No wonder we get stressed: most of our glasses are more than half-empty. As a character in a novel by Thomas Dixon put it: 'I'm an old man now. I've had lots of trouble, and most of it never happened.'

Change blindness

The good news about the autopilot – that it saves time and energy – applies not only when we're faced with danger, but throughout our daily life. It would be tiresome to have to re-learn to tie our shoelaces every day, so once we've learned how to make the bow, lace-tying becomes a mostly automatic process. Driving a car, walking, riding a bike, speaking and writing, playing a musical instrument, or hitting a forehand drive in tennis – once any skill is learned and practised it can become part of the autopilot repertoire. We don't need to think hard or expend a lot of effort for a routine that we've practiced many, many times. It becomes a habit.

A downside of this efficiency is that when we're doing something familiar, we have a tendency to zone out. And when something unexpected arises, the autopilot often fails to spot it, a phenomenon known as change blindness. In an experiment designed to explore this, researchers set up an administration counter where people would come to fill in a form. When someone asked for the form, the assistant would duck below the counter to get it. Another assistant would be hiding below the counter, and this second helper, who looked quite different from the first, would then get up and hand over the piece of paper. Most people didn't notice the switch.[4]

Have you ever driven down a familiar route with the intention to take a different turn-off? What tends to happen? Many people report that they're so used to going the usual way that they space out and miss the planned new turning, even though they had their eyes on the road.

Again, the autopilot is both hero and villain – although we might have got lost in thought, chances are we didn't veer off the road or hit another car: the autopilot (usually) keeps on driving us safely, even though our mind is somewhere else. At the same time, because we're comfortably driving on a road we know well, our mind wanders and we miss the turning, even though we've decided we want to go somewhere new. We're safe, but we're stuck in an old habit groove.

Sometimes the tendency to over-react and be blind to change may not matter, or even be helpful, but if much of what we do happens on autopilot, how far are we living our actual life? If we're sleepwalking through our days, only shaken awake by often-mistaken perceptions of threat, then we're prone to miss many of the joys of living, experience heightened and unnecessary stress, and be blind to some of the genuine choices we have.

Attention training

So, how can we experience things more accurately and fully? First, we need to learn how to pay attention. It's a bit like having a camera that doesn't seem to be working – if the pictures it takes of your living room are fuzzy, do you go and buy new furniture? Or do you examine the settings on the camera, and how you're holding it?

The camera of the mind is powerful, and yet most of us don't learn how to use it properly. It's astonishing really that we spend so much of our time trying to change our life circumstances and so little exploring how to perceive them with skill. We're constantly rearranging the furniture and then taking disappointing pictures, rarely considering if there's an issue with the lens, or our positioning. We fail to see how leaping around like a drunken monkey affects our framing. This is madness, and yet it's how most of us live our lives, most of the time.

If we want to enjoy greater happiness, we need to find another way. But how do we do this when we're stuck in our ingrained habits of perception, maybe without even knowing? It *is* a little tricky, but fortunately, it's also possible. We may not always use the mind's camera well, but it does have the features we need.

Although we're prone to slip into 'monkey mind', our attention *is* sometimes held on a task or other object. There are times when we feel more focused on and connected to what is happening – when we're playing a sport perhaps, or making a meal, or painting. At these times, often when we're doing something we enjoy or feel good at, present-centred attention is happening, and we feel in flow with what we're doing.

We're also capable, to a certain extent, of choosing our course – as humans, we don't live completely on automatic pilot. We may get stuck in self-defeating habits, but we also have some capacity to direct our lives. If we can use what conscious choice we have to practise paying attention, we can expand that domain of conscious choice.

The science of mindful attention

Research is beginning to show the scale of our absent-mindedness, and the tangible effects of paying attention. Matt Killingsworth, at Harvard University in the US, has been running a study,[1] asking people to answer three questions at different times of the day, namely: 'How do you feel?', 'What are you doing?' and 'Are you thinking about something other than what you're doing'? He's collated more than half a million reports from over 15,000 people during 22 activities and found that their minds are distracted 46.9 per cent of the time.

This wandering of the mind isn't harmless. Killingsworth has found that when distracted, people are much less happy than when they're focused (in fact, the study shows paying attention makes more of a difference to happiness than how much money we earn). The link still holds when people are doing something they don't like – a daydream during an unpleasant experience is less likely to bring happiness than staying present to what you're doing, even though you aren't enjoying it.

So, what happens to our attention when we train in mindfulness? Quite a lot, it seems. Many studies have found that long-term meditators perform better in tasks designed to test attention, as do relative novices after they've taken a mindfulness course.[2] This suggests attention is a skill we can learn.

After a few months of mindfulness training, people are more aware of things in their environment that might not otherwise be seen consciously,[3] and experienced meditators are less prone to change blindness.[4] Some benefits of practice can be seen very quickly – one study found that after just eight minutes of mindfulness practice, study participants were better able to pay attention and their minds wandered less.[5]

The effects of mindfulness training can be seen in the brain's attention networks. Both experienced and relatively new meditators show differences in attention-related regions, especially in what's known as the 'default mode network' (so-called because it becomes active, seemingly by default, when we stop paying attention), compared to people who haven't practised. These differences suggest they're able to focus more effectively.[6]

As well as being less stuck in the 'default mode', which has been linked to mood issues such as depression and anxiety, people who practise mindfulness show less 'cognitive rigidity' than non-practitioners. They are more able to be flexible, to come up with creative ideas and new responses, when life throws a curveball.[7] With practice, it seems, we can use our attention to navigate through life.

Attending to the breath

Because the mind is so used to wandering off, a good way to train in attention is to practise placing and re-placing it on a simple object, such as the breath. The breath is a good object for a number of reasons. It's always available – as long as we're alive, the breath is there. We don't have to buy the breath, or remember to take it with us when we leave the house.

The breath's rhythm is the essence of existence, symbolizing a mindful approach to life. The breath doesn't try to get anywhere – it just moves in and out, unfussily engaged in the amazing process of keeping us alive. As with most things in life, we don't have full control over the breath, although we do have *some* influence over it.

The breath happens in the body, and homing to it brings us into centre. We move our place of attending down from the head, where we can easily get caught in worries about the future and analysis of the past. The body is a domain of present-moment sensing, and the breath is always happening in it right now. When we tap into the breath, we may feel our own vitality, our own immediacy.

Attending to the flow of breath can be calming, and as we tune in to it, we may naturally come more into alignment with its qualities of simplicity and steadiness. Even when we feel scattered as we practise mindfulness, the breath offers a reliable anchor to return to, calling us back to attention.

Practice: Mindfulness of breathing

Below are some guidelines for mindfulness of breathing. It's usually a good idea to begin with short sessions of between five and 15 minutes, so you can gradually become familiar with this way of working.

1. Find a place where you can sit comfortably, perhaps on a chair with a firm seat, one that's low enough for the feet to be flat on the floor. Place the hands on the thighs, palms facing downwards. If possible, sit with the spine self-supporting, so you aren't leaning on the back-rest of the chair (unless you know you need extra support). Let the body be upright, but without straining or stiffening.

   Let the head and neck be balanced gently on unhunched shoulders, allowing a sense of openness in the chest. You can close the eyes, or have them open, perhaps letting the gaze fall downwards, a few feet in front of the body.

The overall posture to cultivate is one of quiet dignity, like a just king or queen sitting on a throne. By sitting with dignity, we're cultivating the seeds of confidence and cheerfulness. We're creating a good container in which mindfulness can happen. Notice how this posture feels right now.

2. Now bring attention to breathing. Feel the breath moving in and out of the body – tuning in to its rhythm and flow. Feel the texture of the breath in the belly, and the movements of the abdominal wall with each inhalation and exhalation.

   You don't have to breathe deeply, or try to control the breath in any way – just let the breath happen as it happens. The only task is to feel into and follow it, letting the mind move with it like a surfer riding a wave. Not grasping tightly to the breath, just gently following it in and out.

3. During this practice, you'll probably notice the attention sometimes wandering to some other object. You'll suddenly find yourself thinking about breakfast, or your next holiday, or why your first lover left you. Or maybe your mind will be drawn to a car alarm outside, or a pain in your leg, or into searching for the meaning of life.

4. You might find yourself *thinking* about the breath, or analyzing the benefits of mindful breathing, or telling yourself you're doing this well or badly, or wondering what's going to happen next, or wanting to stop. Or maybe the mind will tell you it's bored. From the perspective of the practice, it doesn't really matter where the mind drifts – you can simply acknowledge that wandering has happened, and patiently, compassionately, bring attention back to breathing.

5. You don't need to berate yourself or see distraction as a problem or failure – each time you notice the mind has wandered, you've already come back to mindfulness. You might like to congratulate yourself when you notice the wandering, and choose to come back to the breath.

It usually helps to time your sessions, as this will give you one less thing to think about. Remember that it isn't the intention to feel calm or relaxed, or to try to concentrate better, or indeed to try to get anything from the practice at all. The only task is simply to feel and follow the flow of breathing, and gently come back when you notice the mind has wandered.

Working with mindfulness of breathing

Mindfulness practice isn't always easy. This isn't a problem: the more we notice difficulty, the more we create chances to gently work with it. Whatever happens when you practise, see if you can cultivate an attitude of 'no problem'. Racing mind? No problem. Falling asleep? No problem. Aching bones? No problem. Restlessness? No problem. In observing these events with kindness, we're allowing space that helps make things workable.

Below are some typical 'non-problems' that people often report when they start practising mindfulness of breathing, and some suggestions for how to work with them.

Frequent thinking

It doesn't matter how many times the mind drifts. The task when we notice is to acknowledge the wandering (perhaps with a mental smile, as if greeting an old friend) and gently return to the breath. As best you can, let go of any judgements (such as: 'mind-wandering means I'm a failure').

There's no need to try and get rid of thoughts – that approach tends only to heighten a sense of struggle. Allow them to be present in the background, and each time you notice the attention wandering to them, acknowledge this and then return to the breath. Remember that each time you notice, acknowledge, and come back from wandering, the muscle of mindfulness is strengthened.

Strong emotions/body sensations

By noticing attachment to pleasant sensations and resistance to the unpleasant, we begin to be freed from their grasp. When you observe that emotions or body sensations have drawn the mind away, acknowledge your noticing with an attitude of kindness, and, as best you can, return to the breath.

Be gentle – if a sensation seems to signal that you need to do something, such as changing your posture to take care of your body, it can be good to listen to that signal and make a shift. Similarly, if emotions or sensations feel too overwhelming to sit with, then it may make sense to stop for a while until you feel a bit more steady, perhaps seeking support from those around you, or a health professional.

Sleepiness/restlessness

Many of us are prey to extremes of sluggishness and excitation. If we frequently fall asleep during meditation, this may be a signal that we're tired and need to get more rest, or maybe we need to practise at a different time of day, when we feel more refreshed. If we choose to continue meditating when we're sleepy, we can open the eyes or raise the gaze, or, as we notice drooping, to re-position the body in a more upright posture.

Restlessness can manifest as twitching, heat, pressure, a racing mind, a sense of irritation and exhilaration, or a strong urge to move. Can you let these experiences pass through you without following or rejecting them, as you compassionately bring your attention back to breathing?

Doubt

This isn't working/It's pointless/I'm wasting my time/I should be doing something more active/productive/ helpful. These are just a few 'practice-interfering thoughts' (the PITs) that commonly arise. When doubt shows up, can you remember your commitment and invite curiosity, allowing these thoughts to move through the mind without automatically believing them? Can you do this just for now, allowing time for the seeds of mindfulness to flower?

Alternatives to the breath

For some people, the breath isn't a stable anchor for attention training, at least to begin with. If you experience hyperventilation or panic attacks, or have a history of breathing problems, it may make sense to start with another object. Paying attention to sensations in the feet (either sitting or walking) or the hands can be an alternative to mindfulness of breathing.

Week 3: practices to explore

- Set aside some time each day for mindfulness of breathing – perhaps five, 10 or 15 minutes (decide how long before you begin, and stick to it, as best you can). See if you can do this without setting any goals to be achieved (such as becoming more focused). Come back to the breath each time you notice mind-wandering.

- At regular points in the day, ask yourself the questions Matt Killingsworth used in his study: 'How am I feeling? What am I doing? Am I paying attention to what I'm doing?' Listen to any answers that come, and be interested in the effect of the questions.

- Notice patterns of absent-mindedness in daily life, and practise mindfulness of breathing when you realize you've drifted. It can be helpful to place a few reminders around the environment to call you back to attention – a sign on your fridge, say, inviting you to pause before you open the door. You could set an hourly chime on your computer to invite you into some conscious breaths (download one at www.mindfulnessdc.org/mindfulclock.html).

- Use delays to help you come back to awareness. Shopping queues, traffic jams, late trains and waiting at home for deliveries are all excellent opportunities to practise mindfulness. In time, you might even start to welcome these delays, rather than seeing them as causes of frustration.

- Choose a different 'C' of mindfulness to work with this week, following the guidance in chapter 2.

Simon's experience

I was brought up by parents who'd say things like: 'Well, that would happen, wouldn't it?' It was a kind of 'the world is against us' approach. Mindfulness has been a significant step in undoing that programming. I think there's a very different way of looking at the world – you don't have to get on the drama triangle every five minutes.

As you grow up, you're programmed to process the world in a certain way, and seeing that is key. Rather than viewing the world as like a jungle where there are snakes and wild animals that can damage you and throw you off track, I now see it as more of a pleasant path through a field. It's not that things don't go wrong, but the way I react to them is very different. Most of the time I'm able to be a calmer, more reflective person.

It's important to experience life in a genuine way: to fully experience being alive, which is a privilege. There are challenges that come with this – I find situations that would have bounced off me before can be more intense and uncomfortable, such as being with insensitive people who are less concerned about how they impact on others – but now I just remove myself from those people when I need to.

Ann's experience

I went to Australia a few months ago and there was so much to do and see. One day we went to the Great Ocean Road. The light was really good for taking photographs, and there were tourists everywhere, bustling up and down a boardwalk. That would have been me before: I'd have been at every vantage point taking pictures, and actually missing the experience.

I used to be so busy that I didn't really see things around me. I was in such a rush that I didn't feel or taste anything. I was just onto the next thing. Mindfulness has helped me realize that I missed a lot.

So this time, after I'd taken a few pictures, I just sat on a bench that had a lovely view and stayed there for 10 minutes, enjoying the moment. It was such a beautiful thing to see, and not just through a camera lens.

Andy's experience

Where we live there used to be lots of cart tracks with deep, muddy holes you could get stuck in. In a similar way, there are probably three or four really boggy cart tracks that my mind goes down, and those tend to be where I'll wake up when my mind has drifted. One is beating myself up about stuff from the past – things I've said or haven't done properly.

Another boggy track I go down is planning – my friends call me the scoutmaster because I'm always making a plan. That can be useful but it can also generate anxiety. We can plan and learn from our mistakes, but we can also beat ourselves up about the past and be really anxious about what's ahead. I call it the beauty and the beast of being human.

I still get negative thoughts, but mindfulness allows me to step back, refocus and respond more kindly to myself. Rather than staying in that deep, boggy hole, I climb out. When I notice my mind wandering, I just say: 'Hey ho, it's busy mind again'.

Mindfulness of breathing helps me settle. I've identified that I have a busy, scatty mind that likes to run at 200 miles an hour, and that's okay. My mind will still run off all over the place, but I can notice it and come back to the breath again and again.

I especially tap into mindfulness of breath in theatres, which still freak me out a little bit. I feel sort of trapped in them, so I do mindfulness of breath to ground myself. I do settle – it takes me probably five to 10 minutes.

Catherine's experience

If you're in the moment, you let a lot more joy in – noticing the flowers or a funny thing your child said, or the sunset. It only has to be a few seconds at a time, but if you can be aware of ten of those moments each day it brings a lot more gratitude.

I still get lost, taken away by my mind, but there are also lots of small instances now where I notice. I just had my lunch and I was reading on my Kindle at the same time. I was like, Hang on a second, let's put it down and notice this cheese I'm eating. *There are lots of little moments like that – I'm more present and appreciative of things.*

SUMMARY

- Working at speed, the mind is on autopilot much of the time. It's taking shortcuts and making guesses, mostly based on past experience.

- By training in attention, we can begin to tame the mind, and to experience things more clearly.

- Each time we practise mindfulness of breathing, we're strengthening the capacity to pay attention.

- Whatever happens when you practise, see if you can cultivate an attitude of 'no problem'.

- Research is showing the scale of our absent-mindedness, and the tangible effects of attention training. We're distracted almost 50 per cent of the time, and less happy when we aren't focused.

- Long-term meditators perform better in attention tasks, as do beginners after they've taken a mindfulness course. The effects of mindfulness training can be seen in the brain's attention networks.

Chapter 4

Opening to Space

'We don't know who discovered water,
but we're pretty sure it wasn't a fish.'

Unknown

With awareness, we can discover a way of being that isn't caught in the reactive jumble of thought, sensation and impulse. If we can distinguish and uncouple our interpretations from our experience, we start to be freed from bias.

What do you notice when you practise mindfulness of breathing? Most people find their attention won't stay on the breath for long. The mind is drawn away, again and again, into thoughts, feelings, sounds, sights, smells – anything but the breath. It's tempting to view this as a problem that mindfulness practice will rectify – if we train ourselves to keep coming back, won't we soon be able to focus more easily?

Perhaps. But something else may be happening too. If you've discovered in mindfulness of breathing that you're not fully in charge of your mind, you might like to ask yourself: *How do I know this? How have I realized that the mind is distracted? And how am I able to bring it back?* In order to notice that the mind has wandered, and be able to return it to attention, there must be something bigger than that mind, a wider perspective that can observe the distraction. That wider perspective is *awareness*.

Seeing with awareness

If I were to draw a V-shape on a piece of white paper, what would you think was there? A lot of people see a bird. Very few people say they see the sky, perhaps with a bird flying through it.[1] We automatically focus on *things*, and we miss the space that contains things.

Awareness sees the whole picture. With it, we can experience life with a more open lens. From the narrow perspective of the autopilot, we might think it's a bad thing to notice the mind drifting, but actually the reverse is true. The fact we can see it means we're opening to greater consciousness.

It's true that in mindfulness of breathing we're cultivating the capacity to attend with greater stillness, stability and strength. But with awareness, we can discover a way of being that isn't caught in the reactive jumble of thought, sensation and impulse, even when attention is drawn to it.

Imagine a cow standing in a very small field, hemmed in by fences. With little space, the animal is stuck – it can't move freely, and it probably feels claustrophobic, angry perhaps, or frightened. Now imagine that the field is made bigger – the fences get moved back, and there's more room to roam. Chances are the cow will be a lot more content.[2]

By opening to awareness, we're expanding the field of perception. Without having to try to change the mind, the very space we offer it can bring release. Instead of being caught in thoughts, sensations and reactions, we find some room to breathe. We can discover a space in which to see what's happening. As it's easier to care for the cow in its more expansive field, so it's easier to handle the wandering mind in the wide-open space of awareness.

We don't have to try to make awareness happen. It emerges naturally from our willingness to disengage from the autopilot and return to the breath. Because we have made a decision to place the mind on breathing, the breath acts as a beacon. We're called back to it when we notice the mind has wandered. Every noticing and every coming back inevitably happens in awareness.

Observing patterns

From this perspective, we can start to see patterns, becoming familiar with whatever tends to come up. What do we usually see? What most people report is that they notice thinking and sensing.

Thinking

In meditation practice, most people notice a lot of thoughts. The capacity for thought is very useful: it enables us to reflect on the past and plan for the future. Thinking in this way seems to set us apart as a species, and many of the great achievements of humanity have stemmed from it.

But as we've seen, thought isn't always an accurate reflection of events: we can misread situations and think things that aren't true. With negativity bias, thoughts can (mis) interpret life darkly: *Why did I say that stupid thing to x? Now they won't be my friend anymore, and they'll tell everyone how awful I am.* When we automatically believe what we think, it affects our mood and behaviour. Our experience of life is skewed.

Because thought is abstract, it takes us into a conceptual mode of processing – one step removed from direct sensory experience. When we get caught up in a concept, it can be as if we aren't really here. We're absent-minded, up in our heads.

Thinking can be a wonderful thing, but when it's our master rather than servant, it can get us into trouble, luring us away from direct experience. Each time we notice thoughts in our practice, we're freeing ourselves from the tyranny of thinking. There is a world of difference between thinking: 'I am stupid', and 'noticing the thought that I'm stupid'. We're discovering that it's possible to relate *to* our thoughts, rather than just *from* them.

Chances are, thoughts will continue to occur as we practise, and we don't have to try to stop them. Noticing them without judgement, we begin to see how we get distracted by thinking. By letting thoughts be as they are, and returning to the breath, we gradually loosen our attachment to thinking.

Neither following nor rejecting them as they pass through the space of the mind, we can see more clearly that 'thoughts are not facts'. They are just thoughts, an aspect of, but not the whole of our being. We can experience the world in a way that includes but is bigger than concept. This realization can be deeply liberating. If we're not our thoughts, then we don't have to react based solely on thoughts that may or may not be true.

Sensing

In mindfulness of breathing, we're paying attention to a *sense perception*: the feeling of breath in the body. As we practise, we may find the mind wanders to other sensory experiences. There might be feelings of pressure, tightening, opening or warmth (for example) somewhere in the body, or maybe we're drawn to external perceptions, such as sights and sounds.

Sensations can exert a powerful pull on attention, especially when they're unpleasant. A throbbing in our back can magnetize our mind – the discomfort dominates and draws us in. As well as the painful throbbing, we may also notice automatic reactions to the sensation – a feeling of contracting in the back or other regions of the body, as we pull in or push away, reacting to the pain.

Let's say while we're practising mindfulness of breathing, we hear the sound of a neighbour's dog barking. We feel a tensing up in our solar plexus, or a clenching in the jaw. Thoughts arise, such as: *That animal never shuts up! I wish they would do something about him – they're really inconsiderate.* The tightening and clenching increases, and is perhaps joined by a sense of pressure at the temples.

In mindfulness practice, we don't have to try and stop any of this. We can notice how we're drawn from our chosen object of attention, such as the breath, and into thoughts and sensations. We can be aware of automatic reactions arising in the mind and body, letting them happen in the background.

In mindfulness of breathing, when we find that our attention has been drawn to thoughts or other sensations, the usual invitation applies – acknowledge the wandering mind, and gently escort it back to the breath. The thoughts and sensations may continue, but we can practise allowing them to be in the background, seeing them from the space of awareness, rather than being caught up in them.

Working with emotions

In meditation, we may often notice emotion. Internal storms can rage and attention is drawn into feelings of sadness, fear or anger. We experience pleasurable emotions too – bliss, joy or contentment.

Emotions are felt in the body – a heaviness or tingling in the solar plexus, a churning in the belly, a pressure at the nose, or a warmth or opening at the heart. Thoughts usually come along for the ride, categorizing the sensation. We feel a dropping in the chest and an urge to withdraw, and the thought comes: *I'm sad.*

Other thoughts might follow: *I shouldn't be sad; why am I sad? I'm sad because my partner left me – I'd better go and find another one.* As well as the sensation, there may be an urge to react – anger arises (as an energy in the chest, for example) and we feel an impulse to attack. Like thoughts, emotions are often driven by previous experience. Whether we feel anger, sadness, fear or contentment seems to be influenced by implicit memories of previous, perhaps similar situations.

Just like thoughts and other sensations, emotions occur whether we want them to or not. In mindfulness practice, we notice these feelings and the thoughts that come with them. If we find it helpful, we could perhaps say to ourselves, *Ah, heaviness in the solar plexus – I call this sadness*. With this practice, we're observing (and labelling) our experience, rather than automatically identifying with it.

How awareness helps with low mood and anxiety

If we have a strong negativity bias, we're more likely to believe that events are out of control: that we're incapable and others are hostile.[1] Seeing threats all around, the autopilot mind can spiral into a self-perpetuating cycle of worrying thoughts, looping round and round, stuck on high alert.

The more this happens, the more negativity bias is reinforced, and the less of a trigger it takes to trip us into rumination and reaction – we forge ourselves a fearful groove. This can lead to depression, anxiety and other mood disorders,[2] which become ever more likely with each recurring episode.[3]

Patterns of automatic thought and sensation become ingrained over the course of a lifetime, and over the lifetimes of our ancestors – we can't simply decide not to have them. This is why crude attempts at positive thinking may not always help: we find ourselves denying or fighting the reality of experience.

Discovering an awareness that isn't caught in autopilot, we can see thoughts and sensations for what they are – automatic reactions that may or may not accurately reflect a situation. In mindfulness practice, we notice our tendency to be caught in the autopilot, and gently disengage. We let go of fuelling habitual patterns.

People prone to depression and anxiety can get caught in negativity bias, and mindfulness seems to help. Studies show that practising mindfulness is more likely to help alleviate or regulate low mood and anxiety than rumination or suppression strategies. After mindfulness training, people ruminate less and are more able to see from a place of awareness.[4]

They're less likely to get stuck in negativity bias[5] and don't get so caught up in rigid thinking patterns.[6] This doesn't mean that difficult thoughts or sensations don't arise, but their sting can be lessened by recognizing patterns.

In one study, people with a fear of spiders were invited to walk towards, and try to touch, a live tarantula.[7] The participants were divided into groups and given instructions on how to handle their fear, such as telling themselves the spider wouldn't hurt them, or trying to distract themselves from what they were doing. The groups were measured according to how close they got to the spider, how upset they felt and how clammy their hands became.

The people who fared the best were not in the group who tried to reassure themselves, or the distraction group, but the one in which people were asked to notice and acknowledge their fear by saying, as they approached, something like: 'I'm anxious and frightened by the ugly, terrifying spider.' By opening with awareness to what was actually happening, they were more able to cope with a frightening situation.

Emptying the boat

The ancient Chinese philosopher Chuang Tzu gives a useful analogy.[3] If we were on a river and an empty boat collided with ours, we would probably just push it away. But if there were someone in the other boat, we might start to feel upset that our boat had been struck. We might even get angry, shouting at the person who didn't steer out of our way.

When we buy into habitual interpretations of thought and sensation, it's as if we're putting someone in the empty boat. When we experience those same thoughts and sensations without getting caught in them, we empty the boat. There might still be a collision, but we probably won't get so upset about it.

If we can uncouple our interpretations from our experience, we start to be freed from bias. If an unpleasant sensation arises, can we treat this as information, without adding to the discomfort with furious rumination or resistance? We don't have to discard our interpretations, but we can know when we're making them and see them for what they are – opinions that we're adding to the basic events.

What are the people like in this place?

There's a story of a wise woman who sat at the gates to a village. A traveller came to the gates and, wondering whether he might come to stay, sought the view of the wise woman. 'What are the inhabitants like here? Are they friendly or hostile? Will they make me feel welcome?' he asked.

'What were the people like in the last place you stayed?' asked the woman. The tourist scoffed: 'Oh, they were a horrible bunch – miserable and stupid.' The wise woman smiled and replied: 'I think you'll find the people here much the same.'

We tend to see the world as *we* are, not as *it* is. By noticing from a space of kindly awareness, we can perceive more clearly our habitual patterns of perception. We start to see that thoughts are just thoughts, sensations just sensations, sights just sights, and sounds just sounds. We can choose to take these as the basis for interpretation, or we can decide to experience them as interesting phenomena that arise in the mind and body.

Either way, by noticing and getting to know our patterns, we untangle from the bind of automaticity. This process is usually a gradual one. We need reminders to come back to awareness again and again. These reminders to wake up are built into mindfulness practice: over time, as we train, we *can* shift from a place of unconscious habit to a place of clear seeing. This shift can be allowed to happen gently – one breath at a time.

Practice: Taking a breathing space

This three-step breathing space practice[1] can help us come into awareness, wherever we are. It can be dropped into the day at any time, and may particularly help when we feel stressed, which is often a cue for the autopilot mind to kick into gear, and we're more likely to be driven to habit reactions. It's best not to see the breathing space as a relaxation exercise, as this creates expectation. The intention is simply to bring consciousness to what's happening right now, in the mind and body.

Step one: Acknowledging

Settle yourself in a dignified posture, as if starting a mindfulness of breathing session.

Notice what thoughts are happening – what's going through the mind? Do thoughts seem heavy and charged at the moment, or lighter, more like they're fluttering in and out? Are thoughts happening fast or slow; are there lots of them, not many, or none? Acknowledging the thoughts, you might say to yourself: Ah, this is what's going on in my mind at the moment.

Bringing your attention now to emotions – is joy, sadness, fear or anger present? What are the actual sensations? Where in the body are you feeling them? Are they changing from moment to moment? Are they increasing or decreasing in intensity? There's no need to try and change what you're feeling – allow yourself to experience.

Now turn your attention to other body sensations. Maybe there's aching, or restlessness, numbness or tingling happening within? Where do you feel these sensations? Be interested in what you find, letting go, for now, of evaluations.

Step two: Gathering

Let thoughts and sensations drop into the background, and gather your attention to the breath in the belly. Rest your attention on the rhythm of breathing – feel the expanding and dropping of the abdomen as the breath flows in and out. When you discover the mind has drifted to thoughts or other sensations, let these be and gently return to the breath.

Step three: Expanding

Open your awareness to the whole mind and body. Let thoughts and sensations be experienced as they are, without having to identify with, change or reject them. Just let them be known with curiosity and compassion.

Week 4: practices to explore

- Practise the three-step breathing space a few times a day, for a few minutes each time. You may like to set an alarm to remind you.

- Continue to work with mindfulness of breathing, bringing a particular interest to how the mind wanders. Notice its patterns – are there certain types of thoughts or sensations that the mind gets drawn to more often?

- Notice one pleasant moment each day and bring awareness to thoughts and sensations that arise with it. Writing down the events, thoughts and sensations can help you see them from an observer's perspective. What happens when you notice pleasant events in this way?

- Also bring awareness to one unpleasant moment each day. What thoughts and sensations arise in relation to these? What effect, if any, does noticing thoughts and sensations have on your experience of events?

- Be interested in your interpretations. When making a judgement, especially if you're in a rush or feeling stressed, you might like to stop for some mindfulness of breathing, or take a breathing space. Ask yourself: *Is this interpretation I'm making based on what's actually happening?* Notice what answers come up: be interested in these too.

- Choose a 'C' of mindfulness to work with this week, following the guidance in chapter 2.

Simon's experience

For me, a light bulb moment was realizing there's a moment in space between an external event and the way you react to it. You can actually have some impact and control over that reaction – if you can be aware of the thought that comes in first. You can start inserting awareness between what's happened externally and how you react inside. Then you can change your whole perception.

Mindfulness creates a sort of contact feedback loop that tells you how you're feeling about a situation, perhaps spotting a little bit of anger here and a little bit of tension there. It's like having a magnifying glass on your insides.

Ann's experience

The practice has been slowly changing how I think about things. It's given me time and space, as well as a framework. I never gave myself that before because I always had to get on to the next task, or I was too tired. I'm quite impulsive in saying: 'I'll do this or I'll do that', but now I have more courage to say 'no' to people. I'm learning to stop myself and look at things from a wider perspective, perhaps asking: 'Can I do this, or do I want to do it, or is it going to help?'

Andy's experience

Often, when you're depressed or anxious, it isn't just the content of what's happening that maintains the depression or the anxiety, it's the process. It's like having a broken washing machine: what you put in the washing machine isn't the problem, it's that the machine needs fixing. Mindfulness is an opportunity to step back and look at the processes in life, at how we actually perceive inside, rather than always looking out.

Some people think meditation is going to be a perfect tranquil state, with a clear mind like a clear sky. Well, I get a lot of clouds running across my sky. But it's about being able to disengage from them, and from the busy mind. It's allowing yourself to have a busy mind as well – being kind to yourself.

Catherine's experience

If you're able to be aware of how you're thinking, you can stand back. It gives you a moment of pause. If you notice you're feeling a certain emotion then it doesn't affect you as much; you're kind of one step removed from it. Part of you may be feeling really angry, but then another part is aware, and you can say: 'I'm going to go and calm down.' If you notice patterns, you can change things.

If you really want to have a bar of chocolate and you say: 'I'm thinking that I really want a bar of chocolate,' you've got awareness that it's just a thought. It's not a truth; it doesn't mean that you must have it. This gives you that little bit of distance. You might still have the chocolate, but after 10 times, you might not. I've learned, with practice, that I don't have to identify with thoughts in my head – they're just there and it's my choice whether to jump on them or not.

SUMMARY

- Awareness is a way of seeing that isn't caught in thought and sensation. With awareness, we can start to see the patterns of autopilot mind.

- Each time we notice thoughts in our practice, we're freeing ourselves from the tyranny of thinking.

- With mindfulness practice, we can work gently to separate experience from interpretation. We do this simply by noticing sensations, and the thoughts that arise with them. This starts to free us from bias.

- Studies show that practising mindfulness is more likely to help alleviate or regulate low mood and anxiety than rumination or suppression strategies.

- The three-step breathing space practice can help us come into awareness, wherever we are. It may particularly help at times of stress, when we're more likely to get caught in automatic reactions.

Part III

BEING WITH...

'The curious paradox is that when I accept myself as I am, then I change. We cannot move away from what we are, until we thoroughly accept what we are. Then change seems to come about almost unnoticed.'

CARL ROGERS

Chapter 5

Staying Embodied

'Much of the insanity of the world comes from people not knowing what to do with their feelings.'

JACK KORNFIELD

If we want not to be drawn into automatic reactions, we need to rehearse our ability to stay present, not just at a cognitive level but by working with our whole bodies. By bringing the mind into the body, we create the possibility for true healing (meaning: 'wholeness').

Hark! The cannon roars

An unemployed actor finally lands a speaking part. He only has one line in the play: when he hears his cue, a loud bang from off-stage, he must put his hand to his ear, look up and declare: 'Hark! The cannon roars.' The director of the show says the role is so simple that the actor doesn't need to attend rehearsals. Nevertheless, realizing this could be his big break, he practises his line over and over again.

Lying in the bath, walking down the street, and riding on the bus, the actor repeats over and over to himself: 'Hark! The cannon roars. Hark! The cannon roars', determined to get his delivery right. The first night arrives and he stands in the wings before his scene, still nervously mouthing his line. At last, his big moment is upon him. Right on cue, he hears the most enormous bang, immediately behind him. Leaping up in terror, he screams: 'Oh my God, what the f*** was that?'[1]

Fight or flight

The fight or flight mechanism is activated when perceived threats arise, and it can't be turned off by thinking about it, or imagining how we *should* respond. When it occurs, stress sets off automatic reactions in the body – hormones like adrenaline and cortisol are released, muscles tense up for action, the heart beats faster and blood pressure rises. We become hyper-vigilant, primed to attack, hide or run.

All this happens without our conscious choice – primed by evolution, the body senses danger and reacts immediately, urgently and unconsciously. When it comes to stress, we react like animals under attack.

Being present at rehearsals might not have prevented shock at the cannon on the actor's first night, but by choosing to practise with the experience again and again (rather than just imagining it), he might have become familiar with the feelings it produced. This might have given him the composure to say his line as planned.

When we remain still and follow the breath, choosing not to follow the powerful dictates of thought and sensation, we are rehearsing being present. Although we may feel the impulse to resist what's happening, or grasp for solutions, we train in not being blown about by every wind. We watch what's happening and gently unhook from the powerful energies that impel us. As we practise this again and again, working with the actual sensations in the body, gradually we can develop steadiness.

Practice: Body scanning

Body scanning trains us in skilful connection to physical form. By attending to different parts of the body in turn – feeling whatever we're feeling in them – we get to know and be with experience as it appears in the moment. We tune in to our 'felt sense', uncoupled from the thoughts that seduce attention away.

Below are some guidelines for practising a body scan. The whole session could take between three and 45 minutes, although practising for around 20 minutes is probably good to begin with.

The body scan is best practised at first using audio guidance, rather than by directing ourselves, which can draw us away from experiencing and more into thinking and self-talk.

1. Find a quiet place where you can lie down comfortably, perhaps on a yoga mat or a rug on the floor; cover yourself with a blanket if you like. Close your eyes if that feels okay for you.

2. Notice the body being held by the ground below. Allow yourself to feel this support, bringing awareness to sensations of the body in contact with what you're resting on.

3. Make an intention for the practice. Remember that the goal here isn't relaxation, or even trying to 'achieve' mindfulness. You are allowing some space and time to bring your mind into the body – to

notice what happens, and to gently escort the attention back when it wanders.

4. Spend some moments in mindfulness of breathing.

5. Directing your attention to the feet, allow sensations here to be felt, just as they're happening right now. This might include tingling, pulsing, touching, itching, warmth, coolness, or something else: feel whatever is here for you, letting go of trying to make anything different.

    Notice where in the feet you feel sensations – in the toes, the instep, the sole, the heel? If there's no sensation in parts or all of the feet, what's that like? Remember there are no right or wrong things to experience – the task is just to feel whatever's here.

6. When you notice attention wandering, as it probably will many times, be interested in where the mind has drifted to, and return to sensations in the feet. Notice any judgements that arise, and, as best you can, let these be in the background of awareness – along with thoughts, sounds, or sensations coming from other places in the body.

7. Experiment with breathing into the feet on an in-breath, and breathing out from the feet on an out-breath, synchronizing this with the actual rhythm of breath in the upper body.

    Move attention now to the ankles and lower legs. Notice what's happening in the muscles, the flesh, the bones. Could you experiment with breathing in and out of the lower legs – being curious about what happens when you practise this?

    Now bring a warm, open-hearted awareness to sensations at the knees and upper legs. Continue to practise working with mind-wandering and breathing in and out of the regions selected. Be interested in any changes in sensation – does what you feel stay the same, or does it shift in intensity or quality, perhaps quite subtly?

8. Gradually, carefully and gently let your attention travel through the rest of the body – the pelvic region and bottom, back and shoulders, arms and hands, belly, sides and chest, neck, throat and head, experiencing each in kindly awareness.

9. As you practise, notice patterns of trying to grasp, ignore or push away. Let thoughts be in the background, neither buying into nor rejecting them. Come back to body sensation when you notice attention wandering.

10. Close the practice by spending some time opening to sensations in the whole body, letting them be experienced as they are, with interest. You could practise having a sense of breathing with the whole body, synchronizing this with the rhythm of actual breath as it flows in and out.

Suggestions for the body scan

*   **Accepting whatever comes up** There's no right or wrong thing to feel when you practise the body scan, or any other mindfulness practice. Whatever you notice is valid, because that's what's happening. Whether you notice thoughts that you're not doing it properly, or you're falling asleep, or there's tension or discomfort, or lots of mind wandering, boredom, irritation or numbness, that's all good noticing. The task is to know and be present to what's here rather than judging it, or trying to change it.

- **Being interested and friendly** As best you can, bring curiosity and compassion to your practice. Many of us wish our bodies were different, or that we didn't feel uncomfortable or restricted in them. As best you can, gently connect to the present moment reality of body experience – even if you don't feel good – knowing that you're offering your body care simply by attending to it. For now, let go of trying to change anything.

- **Not needing to relax** The body scan isn't a relaxation exercise. By setting it up as relaxation we're creating an expectation for how the experience should be. If relaxation comes, that's fine, but so is tension or frustration, or agitation or discomfort. Can you offer compassion to all kinds of experience as and when they appear?

- **Not striving** The only thing we're working to achieve here is awareness of what's happening right now. If other benefits come, they'll most likely come in their own time, as a by-product, not as a result of striving for them.

- **Working with sleepiness** People sometimes drift to sleep during a body scan practice. This isn't wrong – maybe sleep is what your body needs right now, especially if you're tired. If you consistently fall asleep during the practice, you might like to come back to it when you've rested, perhaps practising at a different time of day, or sitting up, or with the eyes open – all of which can help you to 'fall awake'.

Stress and the human animal

Our human capacity for awareness enables us to work consciously with stress. As well as the more primitive limbic system in the brain, which is strongly implicated in 'fight or flight' reactions, humans have larger pre-frontal cortexes than other animals, and these regions seem to be particularly important in working to manage autopilot reactions.

But our greater consciousness also creates some problems. Our bigger frontal lobes enable us to reflect and plan, and when stress occurs we're often driven to think about it, perhaps reliving stressful situations over and over in our minds as we work out what we could do differently. A certain amount of reflection and planning is helpful, as we consider how best to manage our problems, but if there's no obvious fix available, we may just ruminate over and over, the problem kept alive in our heads.

As we keep on churning things over in the mind, we're likely to stay on hyper-alert, as our attempts to solve the problem keep us focused on the sense of threat, and the fact that it hasn't been resolved. The anxiety becomes self-perpetuating – with unfortunate irony, our attempts to find solutions to stress actually keep the feeling of stress alive.

This issue is made worse because many of the stressors we face in our lives *aren't* acute survival threats. In the animal world, a predator attack might last a few minutes, after which the prey either gets eaten or escapes. If it survives the stressor, most animals will settle quickly back into a non-stressed state, the body calming down and returning to balance.

As humans we more often face chronic, lower-level problems – like traffic jams, irritating neighbours, muscle pain, or an overload of emails. Unfortunately, the animal in us doesn't distinguish between these kinds of stressors and the lion that wants us for breakfast, and so the same *unconscious* reactions are set off.

Because chronic stress doesn't resolve easily, and because we're driven to keep worrying and ruminating, even when there's no solution at hand, the fight or flight reaction starts to become maladaptive. We feel tense *all* the time; we get tired from lack of sleep; and we stay on hyper-alert, perhaps over-sensitive to any small problem.

Modern human experience is set up for chronic stress, but we haven't evolved to cope with it – indeed, with our seemingly unique capacity for thought, we're wired to get stuck in fight or flight. This is why, to paraphrase the memorable title of Robert Sapolsky's book, zebras don't get ulcers and people do.[2]

Even worse, the more we get stressed, the more we tilt our brains in the direction of reactivity and negativity bias. Neuroplasticity works both ways – everything we practise becomes a habit. The more we react unskillfully to stress, the more prone we are to get stressed, and the less able we are to choose our response. Overload leads us into greater automaticity, to more unconscious reactions and to more suffering.

When we get stressed for prolonged periods, we may become prone to anxiety disorders, depression, chronic fatigue, hypertension, irritable bowel syndrome, heart problems, diabetes, reduced immune response and any number of other mind-body disorders. We might develop addictions to substances, or behaviours that promise short-term relief from our stress but which end up stimulating further craving for the pleasurable 'hit'. In our brains, bodies and minds, pathways are forged that lead to unhappiness.[3]

The two arrows

When talking about stress 2,500 years ago, the Buddha used an analogy to describe our predicament. In life, he said, we're struck by two arrows.[4] The first arrow represents all the inevitable pain we experience. This might include unpleasant sensations related to getting older or falling sick, as well as the discomfort that comes with other situations that haven't worked out the way we'd like – the frustration of a career dead-end, the sadness of a failed relationship, the anxiety that accompanies financial uncertainty.

It also includes the unbidden thoughts that are sparked by these situations, perhaps repeatedly reminding us that things aren't going the way we want, and telling us that something must be changed to fix the problem. We don't consciously choose these unpleasant events, sensations and thoughts, and once they're here, we can't prevent them happening.

The second arrow, said the Buddha, represents how we *react* to the first one. When we experience an unpleasant event, most of us try to resist it, and/or run from it. This represents our habitual reactions to 'fight or flight' – getting caught up in, or trying to stop, the powerful thoughts and impulses that drive us to deal with the stressor: to 'sort out the problem'.

If we get sick and there's no easy cure, we may be stuck with chronic pain. When we're hurt by unkind words, we may feel an anger that lingers. Perhaps we find ourselves obsessing about what we should do, or why our current strategies aren't working. We step up our focus on the pain or anger, and how to be rid of it.

Or maybe we tell ourselves there's nothing we can do, and instead get frustrated with our thoughts and sensations, which don't seem to listen to reason. We get stressed about getting stressed, turning the fight in on ourselves.

So what can be done? Of course, the best result would be not to experience the misfiring mechanism, but as the actor's tale shows, the fight or flight reaction can't be shut off easily. However, we *can* choose to practise staying present to thoughts and sensations, by noticing how automatic stress reactions arise in our bodies, and how we tend to resist or identify with them.

This might not make them go away, but it significantly alters how we experience them: the meaning we ascribe them, the degree to which they control us, our way of relating to them, and our response. Instead of running round screaming, 'I've got to get rid of this anxiety – *now!*', we might bring a friendly interest to sensations of stomach churning, and the thoughts that come along with it. Staying present to thoughts, sensations and automatic reactions we shift our relationship to stress.

Stress and the science of mindfulness

Science shows the value of responding to stress in this way. Studies have pointed to changes in patterns of brain activity when people start practising mindfulness. The amygdala (a marker of the fight or flight reaction) becomes less active and reduces in size, while there's more activity in regions of the pre-frontal cortex, associated with the ability to regulate thoughts and sensations.[1]

There's less going on in the default mode network of the brain, which is associated with rumination,[2] and more activity in experiential networks, including areas such as the insula, which is active when we tune in to body sensations.[3] There are patterns of greater connectivity between brain areas related to attention and regulation.[4]

Levels of cortisol[5] and inflammation in the body[6] are reduced. The immune system is strengthened.[7] Telomeres, which protect our chromosomes from damage and are shortened by stress, show greater signs of resilience, potentially offering protection from premature ageing.[8] Mindfulness of breathing activates the parasympathetic nervous system,[9] which helps the body come down from the fight or flight reaction – heart rate and blood pressure drop.

People's experience changes too. Mindfulness practitioners are less likely to be negatively affected by stressful situations and react in harmful ways, such as by acting on urges to addictive behaviour.[10] They're more able to regulate mind and body consciously in the face of stress.[11] They can choose to stay present, rather than being driven by impulsive and automatic reactions. They're less prone to firing the second arrow.

To stay present, we need to really get to know the signs of stress, and our habitual ways of reacting to them, as they manifest in our being, again and again. We need to practise staying embodied. Fortunately, there are further means we can employ to cultivate mindfulness of body.

Practice: Mindfulness of body

This practice offers space to experience body sensations fully, openly and with awareness. We become aware of signs of stress in our bodies, and learn how to work with them skilfully. Practise for between five and 20 minutes, or however long feels appropriate for you right now.

1. Settle into a dignified sitting posture, and practise mindfulness of breathing for a time.

2. Open up awareness and notice sensations in the whole body. Be aware of contact – texture and temperature in parts of you touching the floor, chair, clothes, other body regions, the air around – as well as internal sensations, such as tightening, relaxing, pressure, fatigue, heat, cold, aching and so on.

3. As best you can, bring interest to pleasant and unpleasant sensations, feeling them fully. Be aware of preferences – liking some sensations and not liking others – and notice when and how you're getting caught up or resisting. Be curious about any changes in location, intensity or quality of sensation.

4. When you see the mind wander into thinking, bring awareness to this shift, gently letting go of thoughts and coming back to feeling. When you notice the mind wandering elsewhere (e.g. to sounds), acknowledge this also, bringing it back, as best you can, with kindness.

5. If the mind feels very scattered, or sensations are particularly intense, you could come back to mindfulness of breathing for a time, using the breath as an anchor for attention once more. Open up to the whole body again as you feel ready. Perhaps imagine that you're breathing into and out from the entire body.

6. After you've practised, experiment with staying present to body sensations as you move into whatever comes next in your day.

Mindfulness as bodyfulness

There are many good reasons for practising mindfulness of body. We live in a society that exhalts thinking – our education system prioritizes academic learning, and most people are trained when they're young to identify with thought. Even the English word 'mindfulness' makes our subject sound like a quality of thinking. Whereas actually, mindfulness brings us down from our heads and into our whole bodies.

Ask someone from Tibet where their mind is and they may point to their chest – the word for mind and heart in Tibetan, and many other Eastern languages, is the same. When we practise mindfulness, we're recalibrating our centre downwards – as such, the practice might better be described as 'heartfulness', or even 'bodyfulness'.

Whether we recognize it or not, our experience of life is embodied. As the actor's tale shows, the body's reactions are governed by a strong animal sense. We can't just decide not to feel what we're feeling – body sensations are driven at a level deeper than thought. When we come to terms with this, we can let go of trying to force ourselves into changing how we feel by thinking about it. By bringing attention to sensations in the body, we might learn how to work with them skilfully.

To return to the analogy of the rider and the horse, a good relationship is established not by the rider trying to beat the horse into submission, or ignoring its needs, but by listening to it, feeling it, gently synchronising with it. By tuning in, we can notice how the body feels. Using this information can help us – we can start to live a fully embodied life.

The human body is a staggeringly wonderful thing, and yet we so often take what it does for granted – we move around, carry things, make things, see, hear, speak, feel and taste, often without appreciating how this all happens. When things feel right with the body, we take it for granted. When things feel wrong, we get frustrated. And yet, just by breathing, the body is performing magic every moment. Alive, the body is a miracle. This is true, even when it's not feeling how we'd like it to feel.

The body is always in the present. When we take our attention to it, we're naturally drawn to the here and now. Through the body, we can feel the sensational joys of living, beneath the dulling layers of concept that can cloud their vividness. Attending to the body also has a grounding effect. When we bring awareness to the body, we're getting down to Earth. Unlike thoughts, which have no corporeal existence, the body has form. It offers a good counterweight to the flighty mind that's continually zooming off into past and future.

The body experiences by feeling, so by becoming familiar with patterns of physical sensation, we can more easily work with them. If our body is in pain and we try to ignore it, resist it or ruminate on it, we're trying to live outside physicality. This is a recipe for fractured living. The body *is* our home, even when we don't like the state of it. We face a better chance of happiness if we can open to the reality of body experience and explore how to be with it, than if we try to control it with thinking, or wish we could find somewhere else to live.

Practice: The mountain meditation

This practice helps us centre, especially in the midst of life's shifting swirls. By imagining and then embodying the steadiness of a mountain, we train in being present to the weather of the world, as well as our own internal weather.

1.   Settle into a dignified sitting posture, as for mindfulness of breathing.

2.   Imagine a beautiful mountain. It could be one you've climbed or viewed from a distance, or seen in a film or picture, or one you've conjured in your mind. Visualize a mountain that for you embodies majesty and magnificence, full of natural wonder.

3.   Notice how its base is grounded in the Earth, and how it rises into the air, unapologetically taking its place in the landscape. Bring awareness to all its mountainous qualities: solidity, stillness, beauty, grandeur. Realize that come day and night, storm and sun, winter and summer, the mountain abides, sitting in its landscape, unwavering, whatever the weather.

4.   Now notice your own mountainous qualities as you practise sitting – feet in contact with the ground, body rising upwards. Like

the mountain, you too can embody stillness, solidity, beauty and presence.

There may be weather going on – events in life, thoughts and sensations, ebbing and flowing in the internal and external environment. Whatever the weather, practise being a breathing body mountain: naturally wonderful without having to do anything. Let the climate of the world touch you – be rained on, shined on, snowed on – and stay present to whatever comes, neither resisting nor running from it.

5. When your mind wanders, come back to the sense of being as a mountain, or if you prefer, let your attention rest on the mountain in your mind for a while, before returning to the felt experience in the body. Let go of the need to feel a particular way – if you don't feel 'mountainous', that's fine, this practice is inviting you to cultivate a quality rather than force a feeling.

6. Remain practising for five, 10, 15 minutes or longer, as feels appropriate to you right now. When you get up, allow yourself to stay tuned to your mountainous qualities. Come back to awareness of them when you remember, especially when stressful events arise.

Practising acceptance

When *trying* to relax, we're subtly (or not so subtly) rejecting our reality, attempting to get into a different state of being. In mindfulness practice, the invitation is to let go of trying to be calm and instead respect what's actually happening, even if that means opening to tension, agitation, pain or fatigue.

Realizing how amazing the body is, and how powerful, we can allow it to have its present moment. With a wholehearted acceptance of the inevitable, tension drops from our bow and the second arrow falls to the floor, unshot.

Relaxation happens not by struggling for it, but by allowing the mind to come into the body. This invokes a peace that doesn't depend on things being pleasant. The body might still feel tense or uncomfortable, and we might still have unpleasant thoughts racing round the mindstream, but we're dropping the attachment or resistance to these mental and physical events.

This changes everything – we're no longer in opposition to what's happening. Rather than always trying to do something about what's going on, we're practising *being with* it. Some action may be advisable in time, but if our activity comes from impulsively reacting to events, thoughts and sensations, we remain in bondage.

Instead, by practising acceptance, we create a gap between experience and reaction, a willingness to dwell in space. This can sometimes be uncomfortable, but it can also free us from the stress of living automatically. As we train in this over and over again, our relationship to experience can change, from unconscious clinging or rejection to gentle acceptance. We develop the ability to work with, rather than against, our patterns.

Week 5: practices to explore

* Practise the body scan once a day this week. Let go of expectations: just do it as best you can and be interested in what happens. Notice any changes that occur. Be aware of judgements.

- Continue to practise mindfulness of breathing each day, and if you like, extend this to include 10 minutes of mindfulness of body practice. Practise the mountain meditation whenever you like.

- Notice signs of stress in the body, being interested in patterns of events, sensations and thoughts. You might like to practise a three-step breathing space, or some moments of mindfulness of breathing or body. It can also be helpful to direct attention to sensations of feet on the floor. Let go of expectations that this will produce a particular result, such as calmness. Notice what *does* happen.

- Notice also sensations of physical contact during daily life. The touch of clothes on your skin, the feel of sitting on a chair, the tap of computer keys on the pads of your fingers, the sensation of the soles of the feet on the floor. What do you feel when you turn a door handle, walk on a pavement, embrace a loved one?

- Choose a different 'C' of mindfulness to work with this week, following the guidance in chapter 2.

Simon's experience

The results of practising on the mindfulness course were beyond what I'd ever imagined. I remember in the first session we lay down and did a body scan and I couldn't believe how calm and relaxed I felt afterwards.

That experience spurred me on – I thought: It works! After practices like the three-step breathing space

*and mindful movement, I found it a lot easier to insert
space into my reaction to things. It's as if it helped
me with an immunity to reacting. After a body scan,
it takes a lot more to get to me than if I haven't done
one. It's easier for me to pause.*

*Sometimes I 'lose it', but I'm aware that I'm losing it as
I'm losing it! Last week my email froze and I thought
some really important stuff on the computer had been
wiped. I temporarily lost my temper, but I immediately
recovered. One of the great things about mindfulness
is that you're allowed to let yourself off these lapses.*

Ann's experience

*It's very important to me now not to make instant
decisions. I have that habit of taking time out in the day
to think things through. I can take myself away and say:
'Give me a minute, or five minutes,' or 'I'll get back to
you in a day or two.' My normal habit is to be impulsive
and go straight into things. I'm learning through
mindfulness that I don't have to do that because I have
that space and that framework. The anxiety levels are
so much less when I do this, and higher if I don't.*

*You notice these things when you start trying to live in
a mindful way. You become aware of what you're doing
– it's very subtle.*

Andy's experience

*Initially, the most important thing for me was dropping
out of my head and into my body – into a sense of
feeling myself. My head is where I tend to spend most*

of my day, either beating myself up or worrying about things that might be coming up. I think I went for years hardly being in the present at all. Formal practices like the body scan, actually focusing on my body, are enough to press a reset button.

Being in the body gives me a sense of 'terra firma', a 'being here right now'. That sense of feeling the air on my skin, my feet on the floor, allows me to settle into myself, to refocus and respond in a different way, rather than just react habitually. That's a great skill because it gives you the opportunity to do something different.

Catherine's experience

Once I'd been practising regularly for a few months, I felt calmer. I was less irritable and didn't need to react immediately if I was angry or something triggered me. I was really able to give it that microsecond pause.

Practising being present makes you more grounded. You breathe, and feel: This is where I am, *which slows everything down. You feel more contented and at peace, so maybe there's not so much conflict or busyness going on inside you. In that state, it's easier to deal with things, as opposed to when you're in that stressed-out mode; when you're just reactive.*

SUMMARY

- In order not to be drawn into automatic reactions, we need to rehearse our ability to stay present.

- Our experience of life is embodied. Attending to the body brings us into the here and now.

- Body scanning trains us in skilful connection to physical form. It also strengthens stability and flexibility of attention.

- Mindfulness of body offers space to experience sensations fully, openly and with awareness, and to let go of reacting impulsively.

- The mountain meditation helps us cultivate centring.

- Mindfulness practitioners are less likely to be affected adversely by difficult situations, and to react in harmful ways. Brain and body changes indicate more adaptive responses to stress.

Chapter 6

Shifting Towards

*'Don't turn your head. Keep looking
at the bandaged place. That's
where the light enters you.'*

Rumi

If we can approach what's happening with courage, curiosity and cheerfulness, we're developing real power, no longer dependent on circumstances to make us happy. When we make friends with our enemies, we no longer have a reason to fight.

In 2003, at a biotech company called Promega in Wisconsin, USA, a group of employees signed up for an eight-week mindfulness course. At the end, like many people who take such courses, they reported feeling happier and less stressed. However, unlike most people who take a mindfulness course, they also had their heads wired up to EEG machines, which measure brain activity.

The results showed that over the course of the eight weeks, there had been a shift in activity at the front of the participants' brains – whereas before there had been greater activity in the right prefrontal cortex, by the end there was more going on in the left prefrontal region. The shift was strongest in those who reported the largest benefit to wellbeing, and was still evident when the participants' brains were measured again four months later.[1]

This was one of the first studies to associate mindfulness practice with sustained neural changes. It's significant because previous research had shown that when there's more left-sided activity, people feel happier, less anxious, and more able to deal with the challenges of life – they have what's called an 'approach' mentality.

Meanwhile, people who have more right-sided activity in this part of the brain tend to be more fearful, and to shy away from new things – an 'avoidant' mentality. Taking a mindfulness course not only resulted in the participants saying they felt better, the evidence could be seen in their brain's 'left shift'.

What had happened to produce such a change? The course participants had spent two months learning and practising a new way of being. They'd repeatedly trained themselves to manage stress by paying attention and bringing awareness to it – approaching their experience rather than trying to avoid it. As well as attending the course sessions, they practised meditation at home for around 30 minutes a day. Over an intensive period of training, they'd applied the mindfulness prescription to their lives.

Saying 'yes' to the present moment

Once we've developed a foundation of attention and awareness, and are working to stay present and embodied, there's a further step we can take. We can develop our approach mentality, even when things are difficult. Whatever it brings, we can train ourselves to say 'yes' to the present moment, welcoming it in with open hearts. We can move towards experience, even when it feels frightening or painful.

This can sound a little crazy. Who on earth would welcome in pain, fear, angry thoughts, frustration, bad habits or cravings? Let's be clear: approaching the difficult doesn't mean putting your head in a crocodile's mouth, or running in front of a bus. These are the kind of situations the fight or flight mechanism is well designed for, and we can gladly follow its warnings.

We also don't have to go looking for difficulties – life presents enough without our having to seek them out. It doesn't mean we should allow ourselves to get walked over, or invite situations of abuse or neglect. In these kinds of circumstance, we may need skilful action to remove us from danger. But not all situations are transformed with action. And even if doing something can influence what happens next, sometimes the only thing we can do to shift our experience is to change our way of relating to it.

When we wall off what we don't want to face, it drains our energy and obscures our view of reality. In letting our defences drop, we release ourselves from struggling with the parts of life that we don't like. They seem to call for attention anyway, even as we block them out. As the old saying goes, what we resist, persists. Whether it presents in the form of depression, chronic pain, fatigue, anger or rumination, turning gently *towards* difficulty is a transformative shift that dissolves barriers to effective living.

The science of turning towards

Remember the study in which people afraid of spiders were asked to approach a tarantula? The group that openly acknowledged their anxiety were best able to manage it. They not only turned towards the object of their fear, but towards the fear itself. Although it might feel counterintuitive, the more we gently practise this 'turning towards', the more it seems we're able to handle problems.

In another experiment, people were exposed to a painful stimulus before and after a few sessions of mindfulness. After they'd learned to meditate, the study participants reported a 40 per cent reduction in pain intensity. They also rated the pain as 57 per cent less unpleasant. Their tolerance had increased, perhaps because they experienced the pain as less troubling, and so were less averse to it.[1]

During another study, in which people were asked to label expressions on people's faces (e.g. angry, scared), those who were more naturally mindful showed less activity in the amygdala, suggesting a smaller fight or flight reaction, and more activity in the prefrontal cortex, indicating a greater capacity for regulating emotion.[2] The mindful participants seemed more comfortable with acknowledging troubling emotions on the faces in front of them.

Whether it's spiders that worry us, or pain, or unpleasant thoughts, or unopened bills, or relationships with others, when we avoid difficult experiences that can't be put off forever, problems seem to mount. But when we practise a mindful approach, we open a reservoir for coping that can help see us through hardship.

Perhaps this is why, in great mythical narratives, there are so many tales of the rejected becoming majestic – the ugly ducklings that grow into beautiful swans, or frogs that turn into princes when kissed. Somehow we know the seeds of beauty exist in the unwanted, difficult, and painful things in life, and that we can release their potential by greeting them with love.

This is not easy. It goes against all the conditioning, all the impulses, all the logic which tells us: 'Get me away from this feeling, this thought, this unpleasant experience.' It can bring up all our resistance, doubt and anxiety, and we may be tempted to try and fight or deny these too. When we feel the cold, dark night upon us, the last thing we want is to rest in the open.

But ultimately we've nothing to lose – we're exposing ourselves only to what's here anyway. With the light and warmth of awareness, we offer our attitude as fuel for transformation. When we practise this wholeheartedly, courageously, repeatedly, compassionately, over time we may find that even when our frogs don't turn into princes, we might nevertheless learn to love the frog.

Is such a radical shift possible? Yes, according to practitioner reports over thousands of years, and the new data from brain-measuring technology. However, it requires practice, method and courage.

Practice: Turning towards difficulty

This practice is usually best done in small doses at first, and preferably with difficulties that aren't overwhelming. It's also sensible to have established a stable foundation by practising mindfulness of breathing and body for some time first.

1. Settle into a dignified sitting posture, and practise mindfulness of breathing and body for a while.

2. Notice sensations that seem more unpleasant and difficult to be with – such as aching, throbbing, churning, or tightening. If it feels manageable, experiment with taking your attention to a region of intensity, gently opening to the sensations you find.

   Be interested in the qualities of and changes in sensation from moment to moment – rises or falls in intensity, or shifts in location or texture. If this feels too much, it's always okay to continue with or return to mindfulness of breathing or body, or to stop practising for a time. Gentleness is paramount.

   If you are choosing to stay with the intensity, notice what happens – are there impulses to resist or pull away? Perhaps you find your attention pulled into thoughts? As best you can, include these reactions in your noticing, allowing space for them to be experienced, along with the sensations themselves.

3. If you like, experiment with breathing into the region of intensity, opening to sensations on the in-breath, and softening on the out-breath. This isn't to try and change what's happening, but rather to offer a skilful relationship to it – flowing with it, as we've practised already with the breath.

   You could smile softly, and silently say to yourself something like: *It's okay. I can be with this feeling or thought. Let me experience it fully, in awareness. Let me offer it warmth. Let me stay present with kindness.*

4. Stay with the intensity only for as long as feels manageable. If you like, gently move your attention away from and then back towards the intensity, noticing what happens. After a period of working in this way, you can return to mindfulness of breathing or body, or bring your formal practice to a close.

5. If there are no strong sensations present at the moment, experiment with bringing to mind a difficult situation that's alive for you – some troubling issue or problem that you're working with (it's best not to choose the most challenging thing in your life right now – let it be something that feels workable to bring to mind and experience).

    Allow the sense of the difficulty to enter you, inviting any sensations that arise, and moving attention to them. If lots of thoughts come up, let go (as best you can) of trying to fix or solve the problem. Just notice the patterns of thinking in awareness.

    If you find yourself getting caught up in thought, bring your attention down into the body and any sensations you notice here, or come back to mindfulness of breathing, anchoring your attention to the rhythm of the breath.

Compassionate abiding

Being with difficulty in this way is what meditation teacher Pema Chödrön calls 'compassionate abiding'.[2] Staying present to what ails us, we allow ourselves to notice, approach and fully feel what's here, offering a tenderness of heart to what we may formerly have demonized.

It's important not to create expectations. As soon as we're moving into the difficult with the hope it'll disappear, we've turned away from an intention simply to befriend what's present. If nothing happens when we practise, then we can befriend nothing happening. If resistance comes up, we can befriend resistance. If there's anger and pain, or anger at pain, we can feel that intimately, without holding on to it or rejecting it, or buying into stories about it.

If we feel we're failing even at befriending, that too becomes something to embrace with compassion. It's okay to be with whatever comes up, including feeling not okay to be with it. With this radical acceptance, as it's sometimes called, we're no longer in opposition to life. We have put out the welcome mat. We have moved into flow with things as they are.

When times are tough, most of us rage against this approach – it doesn't seem right to stop fighting when we hurt. It doesn't feel right to allow our suffering. But adopting the way of mindfulness isn't to deny the value of skilful action – it just means recognizing that the only skilful way to be with *this* moment is to compassionately embrace it, treating it as a trusted teacher.

Opening to the difficult can't be rushed or forced. Sometimes it's best to wait before turning towards, especially if our experience feels overwhelming. Sometimes we need to seek the support of others first – friends, family or a counsellor – to talk with and be supported by. We can accept that sometimes things feel too much to bear – we aren't deficient for feeling flooded. Defences are put in place for a reason, and while they may become unhelpful, they can be honoured and respected for the job they try to do. If we choose to drop them, we can do so gently, when we're ready.

Acceptance and compassion are essential components of turning towards. Without them, the approach can feel like a forced endurance test, a having to 'put up with our lot' that can seem harsh or self-blaming. When we turn towards difficulty with a muttering of 'Just deal with it' or

'Can't you be more mindful?', we're subtly rejecting what's happening, and our feelings about it, rather than engaging warm-heartedly. In mindfully turning towards, we're making an offer of loving connection. This work isn't easy, and it helps to bring with us a sense of self-care. Our hearts are best coaxed to open gently.

The importance of body posture

In our practice, we work to adopt a posture that embodies mindful attitudes. By feeling our feet on the floor, we're cultivating a sense of groundedness. By inviting the spine to rise and our body to be uplifted, we cultivate confidence and wakefulness. By allowing the chest to expand, and letting go of tensing the muscles, we move towards connection and openness.

The posture we adopt seems to be important – there's a link between how we hold ourselves physically and the tone of our experience. In a famous experiment, a group of students were asked to put on headphones and rate sound quality. The researchers said they wanted to check the headphones would work when people were running, so they asked some participants to move their heads up and down, simulating a jog. Others were asked to move their heads from side to side.

Actually, the experiment had nothing to do with running, or even sound quality – the researchers wanted to test whether the head movements affected the students' perspective. They did – when asked to rate the headphones, those asked to nod rated them more highly than the head-shakers.

The voice in the headphones had been discussing proposed rises to tuition fees at the college, and when later asked to take part in a survey about the changes, the head-shakers suggested a much smaller fee rise than the nodders. Simply moving the head seemed to unconsciously influence how the students felt about two very different issues.[1]

There have been many experiments on the effect of body posture on perception and mood. Psychologist James Laird discovered that people feel happier when asked to make facial movements that created a smile, whereas they felt more angry when asked to clench their teeth.[2] In another study, it was found that adopting a strong sitting posture for just one minute increases confidence.[3]

Just as mood and perception affect behaviour, so behaviour affects perception and mood. As the US psychologist William James suggested over a century ago: 'I don't sing because I'm happy. I'm happy because I sing.'

You can experiment with this yourself. Try taking a hunched, slouching sitting posture with your shoulders slumped, head down and arms folded. Now say to yourself: I feel cheerful and connected. Most people experience the posture and the words as incongruent. Now take an upright, dignified posture, and notice the difference. Most people say they feel more energized and confident.

If we take an uplifted and open posture, embodying a willingness to turn towards difficulty with resilience, we're sending a signal to our minds and bodies that this *can* be done, without being overwhelmed.

Week 6: practices to explore

- Work with either the mindfulness of body practice or the body scan each day, experimenting with 'turning towards' difficult sensations and thoughts when these arise, and when this feels manageable for you.

- Continue to practise the three-step breathing space at regular times, and when you notice stress arising. Be aware of urges to react impulsively to stress, and practise staying present with mindfulness, turning your attention towards sensations in the body. Say gently to yourself: *It's okay for me to feel what's happening right now.*

- Pay attention to body posture. Ask yourself: 'Am I holding myself in a way that cultivates qualities of mindfulness: centring, confidence, cheerfulness and compassion?' Let go of self-judgements and be interested in what you find. Experiment with making mindful posture adjustments, and noticing what effect, if any, this has.

- Ask yourself: 'Is there anything I've been putting off in my life, something that needs attention and which I'm avoiding?' If an issue comes up when you ask this question, notice how the avoidance feels and explore possibilities for mindfully shifting towards it. Remember to be gentle – if what's being avoided feels overwhelming, it may be best to start with something smaller. Remember also that approach doesn't always mean action. You can explore how shifting towards feels by first bringing the situation to mind as a difficulty in your meditation practice.

- Choose a C of mindfulness to work with this week, following the guidance in chapter 2.

Simon's experience

If you're signing up for being more aware, you can't be selective and say: 'Well, I'm only going to tune in to the good stuff.' It's important to be aware of what's going on, to feel all the sensations, whether they're painful or not. It's so easy to run away, but if you run away from internal or external pain, then you give it huge power to derail your life and your contentment, because then you're living in fear of it.

If you can move towards it and deal with it, you take its power away. So even if you do need to deal with the more tricky stuff, it's worth it. Mindfulness gives you tools to know how to deal with this stuff. As for the pleasant sensations, bring 'em on.

Ann's experience

I did my first mindfulness taster day when my back was particularly bad. We did a body scan and that was the first time I just focused on the pain. It was painful but I went with it, which is what we were being asked to do. I felt like I was kind of balancing on the pain, and on the rest of my body, and by the end the pain had gone. That was a real light bulb moment for me – it made me think: There's something in this. *I could see how it was related to letting go of habits.*

I was a great one for distraction techniques, where you go and do something because you don't want to think about something else. I tend to confront things more now, because I know they need to be dealt with. On the course we worked a lot on facing things, rather than shying away from them – that resonated very much with me. I've always been one who can cope with the bigger disasters but the little things brought me down. I realized you can confront even the little things. Just because it's a little problem doesn't mean you shouldn't deal with it.

Andy's experience

Some people think mindfulness is a form of avoidance, but there's nothing avoidant about working with difficulty. You can't swerve stuff when it's hard. You can drink, you can take drugs, you can live with your head in the sand – there are all sorts of strategies you can employ to avoid difficulty – but they tend to trap us and be self-defeating.

Now I can actually sit alongside difficulty and pain and it doesn't absorb me 100 per cent, or lead me to go on a bender. Compared to five years ago I feel I'm grounded enough to deal with pain and let myself feel it rather than getting drunk when thoughts are spinning round and round in my head.

Catherine's experience

My default setting is to move away from discomfort. If something's not working I tend to try and change it rather than just being with it. Sometimes you do *have to change things but I automatically think:* Don't go there, let's get away.

It helps to get comfortable with discomfort, being open to accepting what's there. For example, I'm not very good with noise – and I've got three children! Even if they're just chatting and messing around in a jokey way, I find my default is to tell them to be quiet. So I've worked to get comfortable with the noise and often notice that they're actually speaking to each other quite nicely; they're having a bit of fun.

Difficult things are a part of life. It's how we react that's important. If you can treat them in a kind way, it helps you deal with them – it's not as bad. I've found sometimes that if you breathe into tension, it releases it.

SUMMARY

- Once we've developed a foundation of mindfulness, we can start to take an approach mentality, even when things are difficult. We can train ourselves to say 'yes' to the present moment, welcoming it in with open hearts. We can move towards experience, even when it feels frightening or painful.

- Taking a mindfulness course leads to a neural 'left shift', signifying an approach mode that's linked to wellbeing. If we can approach what's happening with courage, curiosity, compassion and cheerfulness, we're developing real power.

- Turning gently towards difficulty is a transformative shift that dissolves barriers to effective living.

- Opening to the difficult can't be rushed or forced. Sometimes it's best to wait before shifting towards, especially if our experience feels overwhelming.

- Acceptance and compassion are essential components of turning towards difficulty.

- There's a link between how we hold ourselves physically and the tone of our experience. In our practice, we work to adopt a posture that embodies wakefulness.

Chapter 7

Letting Go

'The true value of a human being is determined primarily by the measure and the sense in which he has attained to liberation from the self.'

ALBERT EINSTEIN

When we let go, we actually become free to live in peace. Rather than fighting or trying to escape from the world, we can start to recognize and open to it. We can carry our opinions, our relationships, our dreams and our problems with a lighter touch.

The Buddha told a tale about a king looking for amusement. Instructing a servant to gather a group of men who'd been blind since birth, the king presented them with an elephant. Each man was introduced to a different part of the animal, and then asked to describe what an elephant is like.

Every one of the men gave a different report. Touching the head, one man said the elephant was like a pot; another, holding the foot, said it was like a pillar; another, feeling the trunk, said it was like a plough, while one holding the tip of the tail said it was like a brush. The story goes that the men began arguing over the correct answer, becoming so angry they started trading blows.[1]

We (and everything else) are like the elephant in the story – experienced without clarity, things can feel definite and solid, but when we really open our eyes, they appear more fluid. What we see depends on how and where we're looking.

As in the elephant story, stress comes when we cling to views and labels that are based on a limited perspective, rather than seeing the bigger picture. With fixation comes suffering.

Not holding on

In the Buddhist tradition, three hallmarks of existence are described. The first of these is dissatisfaction – there's a stress that seems to come from our habitual way of living. The second is impermanence – things are subject to change, and however hard we try, nothing can ever be made to stay the same. The third is that there's no essential self: no independent entity that we can pin a label on and say: 'That's me'.

The good news is that the first hallmark of existence can be eased, even transcended, by fully realizing, appreciating and shifting into alignment with the second and third. Our stress comes from trying to grasp the ungraspable and resist the irresistible – when we accept that things are impermanent, and there's no essential self-nature, we're liberated to live in accordance with reality, like an undammed river flowing free. There are still difficulties, but by flowing and working *with* what's happening rather than against it, we're less likely to suffer.

The heart of the path of mindfulness lies in this injunction: 'Nothing whatsoever should be grasped at and clung to as 'me' or 'mine'.[2] When we stop trying to hold on, we actually become free to live in peace. Rather than getting caught up in ourselves and treating every misfortune as a personal affront, we can learn to live more lightly, recognizing that things are always in transition. By letting go into this truth, we can experience a happiness that isn't dependent on getting things 'right'. As the Thai meditation master Achaan Chah put it: 'If you let go a little, you will have a little happiness. If you let go a lot, you will have a lot of happiness. And if you let go completely, you will be free.' Every time we drop our fixations, we're able to live in liberation.

Letting go like this isn't easy. As we've seen, our habits of perceiving and behaving are strongly entrenched. Even the idea of non-attachment can seem daunting, impractical, or even undesirable. What about our loved ones – are we not supposed to cling to them? Or our homes – should we throw the deeds away and let anyone come to stay, perhaps trying to live without money or possessions? And where does this leave our ideals – should we let go of aspirations for a better life or world?

Non-clinging is a profoundly alien concept for most of us. Our human history and culture points us to grasping – to our friends and family, to our opinions and feelings, to our belongings, our sense of being an individual, and to life itself. And yet, we could ask ourselves: does this way produce happiness?

The suggestion that clinging leads to unhappiness is not meant as an opinion about morality, or an ideological statement. It's offered as an observation about how the mind, the body and the world work: to be explored and tested in the laboratory of experience. If things are impermanent and there's no essential self to be found, then trying to hold on to material objects or fixed identities is bound to produce suffering. So is it true? *Is* there anything that's truly permanent or independent?

Are things impermanent?

Take a flower. Literally if you can – connecting with an object through the senses helps make this investigation practical and grounded, rather than just intellectual or theoretical. Ask yourself – is the flower staying the same, or is it changing? Is it the same flower as it was yesterday, and will it be the same tomorrow? Is it growing, opening, or wilting? If you took a video of the flower over a few hours and sped up the playback, would you be able to see it changing form?

Now what about everything else around you? Is the home you live in exactly the same as it was 100 years ago, 10 years ago, one year ago, a month ago or yesterday? Is the weather the same as it was this morning, or has it become warmer, cooler, brighter, cloudier, or started or stopped raining? Are the seasons coming and going, rivers rising and falling, bacteria, insects, fish and animals being born, living, dying, even whole species emerging, mutating and becoming extinct? Have the continents shifted position over thousands and millions of years, and do they continue to do so?

And what about *you*? Are you the same person you were 10 years ago, five years ago, one year ago, last week? Do you look precisely the same, have exactly the same ideas, like the same things, or feel the same way as at each of these other time points? Have your perspective and capacities changed – your skill set, vocabulary, opinions, strength and flexibility? Are the thoughts going through your mind right now precisely the same thoughts you were having this time last month, or even a minute ago?

What about body sensations – are they staying the same, or are they shifting, perhaps subtly, from moment to moment? And how about your body itself – are its constituent parts altering, even with each breath as new molecules of air enter and leave? Cells, muscles, blood, skin, bone, vital organs – are these static or in flux, degenerating, regenerating, and mutating?

And what about other people? Are your friends and family getting older, subtly changing what they know, do, or think? If you took a photo of any person once a day for a whole lifetime, would their appearance remain the same in all the pictures? Do countries, cultures and civilizations change? Where are ancient Rome, the Soviet Union or Rhodesia now? Where are the ideas and political systems believed in by the people who lived there?

Now ask yourself: is there anything in the appearing world that *isn't* in transition? Aren't even mountains and oceans subject to shift? Aren't stars – including our own sun – destined to fizzle out? Don't cosmologists tell us that our universe itself is continually changing – whether that's exploding into being, expanding, contracting, or some day imploding? So far as we can tell, there's nothing in the appearing world that isn't subject to ongoing flux.

See if you can connect with this – not just as a thought or an idea but as an *experience*. Can you connect with this as phenomenal truth? Do you notice any resistance to it? Does fear arise? Or calm? How does your body feel? Can you sense this flow of ongoing change or does it feel abstract? Is *this* experience changing from moment to moment too? Are you changing with it?

So *who* are you?

Now, perhaps we might be ready to ask – who is this 'you' anyway? If your thoughts and sensations are changing from moment to moment, along with your physiology, then where is your essential personhood?

When asked this question, many people point to their bodies. But let's say you lose a finger – are you still the same you then? What about an arm? Or a leg? Or both legs? If yes, then are the body parts that have been lost still you? What about if you undergo a heart transplant? Are you still you with someone else's heart? Has the organ donor transferred some of their self to you? If every aspect of your body – muscles, skin, blood, cells – is constantly shifting form, then which bits constitute the *real* you?

Some people might say, 'I am my mind'. So what about those automatically arising thoughts or sensations that you've been watching in meditation? How can they be 'you' if they aren't consciously chosen? What are they doing in 'your' experience?

And what if you suffered a brain injury, and (as can happen) your personality, beliefs and habits underwent a drastic change: would you still be you? If no, does that mean that you were in the part of the brain that was injured? If yes, what would you consider as the traits that define who you are? What if these were the ones lost or changed by an accident? Where is the essence that defines you then?

When we investigate closely, it becomes impossible to pin down something that we can categorically call the self – an independent, unchanging identity. It's not that we don't exist, it's that we don't exist in the way we habitually imagine ourselves – as a solid, fixed entity.

Practice: Mindfulness of breath, body, sounds, thoughts and choiceless awareness

In this practice, we spend time bringing awareness to different aspects of our moment-by-moment experience. Attending to these facets, we may notice how the phenomena that make up life are fluid rather than fixed, as we relate from a place of conscious abiding, experiencing fully without grasping or rejection.

1. Settle into an upright, open sitting posture. Practise mindfulness of breathing for a while.

2. Expand your attention to sensations, practising mindfulness of the body.

3. Now let sounds be experienced in the foreground of awareness (or if you prefer, another sense perception – seeing, tasting, smelling) and allow this to be the main object of mindfulness, coming back when you notice attention wandering.

4. Turn your attention now to thoughts, experiencing these on the main stage of the mind, with everything else dropping into the wings. Observe the coming and going of thoughts in the mindstream, a bit like you might watch clouds passing in the sky. Just as the weather is constantly changing, notice how thoughts arise, pass through and dissolve in the same way. Allow thoughts to be seen with interest, as best you can, neither identifying with them nor trying to stop them.

    Be curious about how this process of arising and dissolving occurs. Have you consciously chosen these thoughts, or are they appearing without your active involvement? Are these thoughts facts, always an accurate reflection of reality, or are they just opinions arising and falling away? Are they even *your* opinions, *your* thoughts? There's no need to analyze this with more thinking, or try to find definite answers – simply let there be noting of what your experience shows.

5. Open awareness now to all aspects of experience, as best you can without preference. Let there be a gentle sensing of sound, sight, feeling, taste and smell, while noticing and accepting thoughts as they pass through the mind. Allow each of these aspects of consciousness be known in awareness, moment by moment, without holding on or pushing away.

    This practice is sometimes called 'choiceless awareness' or 'open presence' – a willingness to experience everything that's happening with equanimity. Whatever is here right now, can you let it *be* here, without having to do anything with it? Can you experience the luxury of just being present? When the mind narrows into one aspect of what's going on, or floats into unconsciousness, bring it back with kindness to this state of open awareness, continuing to rest here for as long as you like.

    Before expanding into mindfulness of thoughts or choiceless awareness, it's often good first to settle with mindfulness of breath, body and sounds. However, as you become more experienced, it's fine to practise just one part of the meditation in any particular session.

Practising mindfulness of thoughts and choiceless awareness are quite different modes of relating to the ones most of us are used to, and so it's important to approach this with compassion. We may find the mind wandering off more than usual. This isn't a problem – we can just keep on noticing, and coming back to whatever aspect of the practice we're working with at the moment.

We can return to mindfulness of breathing and/or body at any point, to help us ground and stabilize our experience, before shifting again into mindfulness of thoughts or choiceless awareness.

A bundle of tendencies

It seems that what we call 'I' is a bundle of tendencies, continually in process, subtly shifting form all the time, according to causes and conditions. The 'I' that exists in the present moment is to a large extent the consequence of what has come before – influenced by the evolutionary history of our species, physiological inheritance from our parents (and their ancestors before them), and what we have learned from our families, friends, schools and wider society (what we might call our psychological inheritance).

The experience of self – our thoughts and sensations – is also influenced by current environment and circumstances – we might have a very different experience watching the waves of the sea on a summer holiday with loved ones, than when living alone in a cold one-room apartment at Christmas, in a city where we know no-one.

We may know all this intellectually, yet it's hard for us to translate into the realization that there is no 'me' as the star of the show. Despite all the evidence, it can still seem counterintuitive, perhaps disconcerting. So we tend to hold tightly to an intuitive sense of there being a definite 'I' in the middle of things. We're tenaciously self-centred.

The science of interconnection.

How we think, feel and behave is deeply influenced by the world around us. We're not separate minds and bodies – it seems that many aspects of our physical and mental being are in ongoing symbiotic relationship with other people and the environment.

Studies have shown that if a close friend of ours is happy, we're 15 per cent more likely to be happy ourselves. If a close contact of that friend is happy (e.g. their partner), we're 10 per cent more likely to be happy. If a friend of a friend of our friend is happy, our chances of happiness are increased by 6 per cent. Each happy person that we have in our life increases our own likelihood of wellbeing by 9 per cent.[1]

Unhappiness is also contagious, and the influence extends to other kinds of feelings and behaviours too – if your friends are overweight, you are more likely to be overweight, and if your friends don't smoke, it'll be easier for you to give up smoking. Having a network of family and friends giving strong social support is known to be associated with increased immunity to infection, lower risk of illnesses such as heart disease, and reduced rates of depression.[2]

One study examined 103 pairs of college roommates who had been randomly allocated to share together at the start of their university life. All the students were assessed on their thinking style, and how it might make them more or less vulnerable to depression.

Over the following six months, it was found that the roommates' thinking styles had converged – those who roomed with someone prone to depression themselves became more vulnerable, whereas those who shared with less vulnerable students became less at risk. This translated directly into depressive symptoms – the students who had higher levels of vulnerability three months into the term were more likely to feel depressed after six months.[3]

In a study to evaluate the power of environment on how we behave, a group of students were asked to take a test of attention. Half were invited to take it while wearing a scientist's white coat, while the other half wore their own clothes. Those students who wore the lab coats made half as many errors as the other group.[4] Another study found that amateur golfers' performance improved when they played with a putter said to belong to a professional.[5]

Influence is also passed down the generations. We might know that our risk of certain illnesses is affected by genetic inheritance, but the new science of epigenetics is suggesting our risk may be affected by the behaviour of our parents and grandparents too.

It has been shown – perhaps not surprisingly – that pregnant rats given nicotine are more likely to give birth to asthmatic pups. However, when they reached maturity those pups were also more likely to give birth to asthmatic rats, even though the third generation had not actually been exposed to nicotine – the nicotine consumption of their grandparents seemed to influence their vulnerability.[6] If the results were replicated in humans, this would mean that a child's risk of asthma could be influenced by their grandmother smoking, even though they might never meet.

Whether in wellbeing, behaviour, or physiology, interconnection runs deep. Knowing this can help us relax into acceptance of our inevitably limited control over current events. At the same time, it can give us confidence that whatever we do and however we are in our lives affects (and potentially benefits) others and ourselves.

The consequences of 'selfing'

If these were merely philosophical questions, then perhaps it wouldn't matter very much. But the assumption of solid selfhood has consequences. It creates a mismatch between our ideas and reality. Things change, and when we aren't prepared for this, it hurts. When resisting the flow of life – railing against getting older, attempting to stop people moving in and out of our lives, or attaching to what we see as the ideal job, house, car, or friendship – we're fighting against nature.

Assuming a single, separate self artificially disconnects us from the world. Although we continue to be part of an interwoven dynamic, we think and feel ourselves more as isolated entities, prone to aloneness, defensiveness, perhaps even aggression. As we try to protect ourselves, we may harden and withdraw rather than open and connect.

In this state, our world can feel small and claustrophobic. There's little space, which means there's not much room for awareness to happen. Because it flies in the face of reality, this hardening, isolating and closing takes considerable energy to sustain. It requires ongoing activation of the fight or flight mechanisms, which are primed to react to change as a threat.

When we deny how things mutually influence one another, we take on a heavy burden of responsibility. If everything that arises in our experience is 'me', then it's a short leap to judging and blaming ourselves for everything that happens to us. It can come to seem entirely 'my fault' that unpleasant thoughts and sensations arise, or that we get sick, or that we've developed unskilful habits of behaviour, instead of being the result of many causes and conditions, some of which we could do little about.

When difficult circumstances happen, we can become super-hard on ourselves – demanding that we sort things out without help. We might embark on all sorts of harsh self-improvement plans, which actually involve firing quivers of second arrows in our own direction. We can get obsessed with ourselves, stuck on what's wrong with us, which may actually increase our unhappiness: it's been shown that people who use the words 'I' or 'me' more often in therapy sessions are more likely to be depressed.[3]

And while we frantically try to change ourselves, an assumption of permanence, of self as solid identity, would seem to preclude the possibility of that change. If current thoughts, sensations, diagnoses or behaviours represent who we are in essence, then surely there's little or no hope of a shift – we're stuck. If this is the case, why even bother working for transformation? It's a pretty bleak scenario.

So it may seem disconcerting that there's no 'me' at the core of our being, but actually it's very good news. As the Taoist philosopher Wu Wei Wu said: 'Why are you unhappy? Because 99.9 per cent of everything you think, and of everything you do, is for yourself – and there isn't one.'[4] We aren't isolated individuals, irretrievably set in our ways, and realizing this can come as a huge relief.

What happens when 'I' let go of 'me'?

If we can accept that things are continually changing, and that we're not single, independent, fixed selves, what are the implications? First of all, it means that we aren't in total control – no matter how hard we try, we can't command our bodies not to age or get sick, and we can't just decide to be happy in any circumstances, or prevent unbidden thoughts or sensations.

We're not in complete charge of our environment either: from unpleasant weather to people we find difficult, there are aspects of our world, internal and external, that we're not empowered to alter. This is a chance to practise co-operation: by accepting this, we can stop some of our struggle with the inevitable parts of life that we don't much like. We can stop taking them so personally.

It's also an opportunity for compassion: we can recognize that we aren't solely responsible for our thoughts, feelings and behaviour, which are each the result of many and myriad causes and conditions in our bodies, brains, minds, and environment. We can let ourselves off the hook, recognizing that the situations of our life haven't always been freely and fully chosen. We can soften to ourselves, and, seeing that the same is true for others, we can soften to them too, even when they do things we don't like or agree with.

At the same time, we can recognize that we're *not* completely stuck. If we're a range of changing processes rather than a single, solid entity, then just because things are tough doesn't mean we're fundamentally broken. No matter what our problems, there's room for manoeuvre.

Our brains can change, our bodies can change, our minds can change, and our lives can change. No matter what's going on right now, pleasant or unpleasant, we can be sure it's on its way to becoming something else.

Accepting that situations aren't as simple or as stuck as we imagine can make them feel more workable, even in the midst of great challenge. By appreciating there are many aspects to any circumstance, we can start to see where the wiggle-room lies – where we have some agency to effect skilful changes. We can also see more easily where it's best to let things lie.

By knowing and accepting present moment realities, we're choosing a skilful relationship with things as they are. We may not have complete control over our lives, but by tapping into awareness – recognizing where the choice points lie – we can use our energy effectively, and helpfully influence events.

As for what we can't control, we might open up to a sense of wonder, realizing how we're only a very small part of a gigantic, interconnected universe (perhaps universes) that we actually know very little about. We could allow some amazement that we're here at all – able to consciously experience our lives, the pleasant along with the unpleasant. Retuning ourselves to this perspective can help us view and experience life differently. We're in a better position to respond flexibly.

This approach of non-clinging, far from meaning that we stop caring about people, actually frees us to truly love them, as our love isn't conditional on their being who we want them to be. We don't have to give up our aspirations: we can move towards them without being hampered by preconceived ideas or by needing things to happen 'our' way. Far from having to reject the world of things or people, we can *really* enjoy them, *really* love them, without grasping so hard, scared of what we might lose. As William Blake said: 'He who binds to himself a joy/Does the winged life destroy/ He who kisses the joy as it flies/Lives in eternity's sunrise.'

Bringing awareness to the process

This is, of course, easy to say, and even perhaps to believe as an idea, but it's sometimes hard to connect with in our hearts. Not only are we used to seeing ourselves as 'our selves', but we continue to feel like a unified 'me'.

How can we tune in to this bigger view? First, we can bring awareness to it. In your brain right now, there are billions of cells communicating with one another, while oxygen is being passed through your body, helping every part of your physical form (made up of billions and billions more cells) keep you alive and functioning.

All of this is happening without your conscious choice, and yet all of it is happening as a vital part of the ever-changing experience of being 'you'. So many events, so many aspects, so much change: all of it 'you' and yet so much of it happening without 'you'. When we realize this, does the concept 'you' make much sense? We can see that we're not our body parts or sensations, we're not our thoughts, we're not our memories, our life stories, our names or nationalities, and we're not our depression, our anxiety, our anger or our pain. While each and every aspect of experience forms a part of the ever-changing process we like to call 'me', none of them need define who we are.

We can notice how easily we revert to making fixed, possessive, black-and-white statements such as 'I'm always in pain' or 'I'm a terribly anxious person,' and ask ourselves, 'Is this really the way things are?' Wouldn't it be more true to say: 'There are painful sensations right now' or 'There's a tendency for churning in the stomach when perceived threats appear.'

We can notice how the very fact of observing these experiences shows they're not the whole of us. We can see that the observer of stress or pain is not stressed or in pain – even when difficulties occur, there is space in our experience that isn't consumed by these problems, as long as we look from a place of awareness.

When we experience difficulties without resistance, then we might not be so upset by them. Pain becomes more workable, manageable; it's not a barrier to happiness, even while it might be unpleasant. Our wellbeing is no longer dependent on the content of our circumstances. This is true liberation.

We don't have to stop calling ourselves 'me', or taking care of the things around us, but we can realize that personhood and possessions are conventions to be observed and experienced, and that this observing and experiencing frees us to enjoy who we are and what we have. This, perhaps, is the real potential for being human.

Solidifying our moment-by-moment experience into 'selfhood' is a habit. Formal mindfulness practice is one of the best antidotes to this – when we meditate, we notice how thoughts, sensations and events are in flux, and how life is made up of many changing aspects.

The science of mindfulness and the self

Neuroscience studies of meditators seem to reflect a changing view that comes with mindfulness. This is suggested by activity changes in the brain's 'default mode network', an attention-related region which, as mentioned previously, is active in most people, most of the time.

It's been shown that when this network is active, the world is being viewed from a conceptual frame – the mind is wandering into thinking, planning, story-making, categorizing, problem-solving and generally making interpretations of what's going on – what's also been called the 'doing' mode. The default network tends to be active when we're viewing life from a 'self-centred' perspective: interpreting events from a sense of how 'I' think about things – my ideas, opinions, and judgements – one step removed from the actual events themselves.[1]

When people move into a more mindful mode of processing – directly sensing events with present-moment awareness – a different set of brain regions, sometimes called the experiential network, comes more online. There is less activity in the medial prefrontal cortex and increased activity in the insula (an area known to be implicated in processing body sensations) and the anterior cingulate cortex (a region associated with the capacity for switching attention). Activity in this 'experiential network' appears to be a marker of the 'being' mode of mind.

After eight weeks of mindfulness training, it seems people are more able consciously to switch their mode of processing from the conceptual to the experiential, to shift from doing to being. This seems to be reflected by the changes in brain activity from the default to the experiential network, which occurs when newly trained meditators are asked to pay attention mindfully.

When people who haven't learned to meditate are asked to do the same thing, they are less able to make this shift, tending to get more stuck in the default mode.[2] Studies also suggest that the default mode network is deactivated more strongly in experienced practitioners (compared to novices), and there's greater connectivity between areas of the brain thought to be involved in self-monitoring and cognitive control.[3]

This seems to be more evidence that practising mindfulness fosters neuroplastic changes that increase the capacity for conscious living. The good news that has been shared by meditation adepts over the centuries, and which has growing validation from scientific studies, is that we can train ourselves to switch from relying on the default mode and into opening to a more mindful mode – we can choose to move from doing to being.

Week 7: practices to explore

- Practise mindfulness of breath, body, sounds, thoughts and choiceless awareness in sequence, perhaps allowing five to 10 minutes for each part of the meditation. Notice what happens, bringing curiosity to how aspects of experience arise and fall away, and what, if anything, changes when you allow this to happen without clinging or resistance.

- Practise the breathing space at regular times, and when you notice stress arising. Bring particular attention in the acknowledging step to thoughts and sensations – notice how they're changing from moment to moment. In the expanding step, allow everything to be experienced in choiceless awareness.

- Bring awareness to the impermanence and interconnectedness of everything in life. Notice how things, people, thoughts and feelings are changing and influencing one another, in dynamic interplay. As best you can, open to a sense of riding with circumstance, meeting life less from a place of independence and isolation and more from a space of connection and co-operation.

- When things become difficult, and stress arises, experiment with allowing this to be seen and felt as part of the dance of existence. As best you can, go with the flow, knowing that both the peaks and troughs of life are subject to change. Notice any automatic patterns of tightening, pushing or solidifying that occur during times of stress, and experiment with allowing these to be felt with compassion.

- Bring awareness to tendencies of 'selfing', trying to turn experience into something rigid. Be interested in your use of personal pronouns, especially in conjunction with words that fix you, others or things into seemingly unchangeable categories (*I'm always depressed/She's a bad person/Why does he never learn anything new?/The traffic is bound to be awful.*) What happens if you connect with a curious, more present-moment-centred view (*There is a heaviness in the belly and self-critical thoughts in the mind right now/Holding on to old habits at the moment/I wonder how the traffic will be today?*)

Does viewing events with less of a sense of fixation change what's experienced, or the relationship to experience? If so, how?

- Be interested in the effect of seeing from a place of awareness. When stress arises, and you notice it, ask yourself: is the observer of the stress also stressed? Or is there a 'seeing' of what's happening that isn't caught up in the experience itself?

- Choose a C of mindfulness to work with this week, following the guidance in chapter 2.

Simon's experience

There's an idea that if you take away all your roles, such as parent, husband or worker, that's who you are. That's had a huge impact on me. Mindfulness helps me see when I'm going back into role identification, when I'm attaching to something. I was attaching to 'our' field at the back of our house – the one I mentioned in Chapter 2 that might be built on. Part of the problem of course is that it's not our field! It 'belongs' to somebody else and we're lucky enough to be able to look at it. I was identifying with the field, even though 'the man with the view' isn't really who I am.

Mindfulness helps me see the little alarm bells when I can feel myself attaching to something, or having a reaction based on an identification, or an identification being threatened. The signs of that are intensity, tension, upset, or anger. Mindfulness reminds me there are different ways of dealing with things.

Ann's experience

In my head I have this role of being the eldest child and the eldest grandchild. It's not necessarily in anyone else's head, but for me it's meant that I've had to act in a certain way and be that person – the one who's always calm and good in a crisis.

But I couldn't always cope with that role; it's not who I felt I was inside. No-one had ever said I had to, but unconsciously that's what I was choosing. I took on that role and actually I didn't want to sometimes – I wanted to scream at everyone to go away!

Part of me likes that role, but I now realize that I needed support not to be the one who's totally in charge. I got wrapped up in that persona. It was very lonely and a great source of stress. Even my work was something I did to have an identity.

Andy's experience

Mindfulness practice changes the experience of who 'I' am. We're the sum of our experience, a collection of molecules, and all types of programming that's developed. There's a biochemical element to us, but I believe we do have choice, to a degree.

It's really useful to be aware of our desires and cravings, as well as what we tend to avoid, because it gives us a deeper insight into the mechanisms that make us operate as beings. Understanding the processes and the reactions within us can give us a much deeper insight into how things impact on us and how we respond.

Our circumstances will funnel us to a degree, but often we can do something different if we want to. We've learned to think as we do because of past experiences, but we don't have to be stuck. Where and how we go in the future is very much down to how we look after ourselves in the here and now. In meditation you get some insight into that.

There are some things I'm not stuck with anymore because I'm relating to them in a different way. Take the anxiety of carrying a cup of coffee across the room. I might think: I'm carrying this cup of coffee and my hand's shaking, and people are going to see me as a weak person. *But hold on: if my hand shakes and I'm a bit nervous when I enter a room, isn't that a normal human experience? Does it really make me a weak person? So now I might think:* Well, if my hand's a bit shaky, that's fine. *And then my hand doesn't shake. By allowing myself to be, I'm already dealing with it.*

Catherine's experience

Sometimes I try to fit myself into too few boxes. I say: 'I am me *and this is what I do; I'm not allowed to do something else.' We have a view of ourselves, and what we can and can't do – how the world is and how we relate to it.*

For about 10 years, I've thought that I want to be more organized. I want to have everything tidy, with routines and a diary, to be in control and to know what's going on. I grew up in houses that were messy and I was labelled as the organized one. But I've been wondering if I'm trying to force myself into a particular way of being as a strategy to cope – actually, I can be a bit more intuitive, creative and 'go with the flow'.

So I'm learning to trust, rather than trying to be organized in a really set way. That means being mindful of how I'm feeling and sensing. It's thinking, What's a good thing to do today? *rather than* What should I do? *or* I must stick to what I'd decided, even though I've got a headache and I'm really exhausted. *It means letting go and giving up control.*

SUMMARY

- There's nothing in the appearing world that isn't always changing.

- We can't pin down the 'self', in the sense of an independent, fixed, unchanging entity. We exist, but not in the way we habitually imagine.

- What we call 'me' is a bundle of tendencies, subtly shifting, dependent on causes and conditions, interconnected with others and the environment.

- Our stress comes from trying to grasp the ungraspable, and resist the irresistible – when we accept that things are impermanent, and that there's no essential self, we're liberated to live in accordance with reality.

- Brain studies of meditators seem to reflect the transformation of view that occurs when we open to a mindful perspective. After eight weeks of mindfulness training, people are more able consciously to switch their mode of processing from 'self-centred' to 'experience-oriented'.

- Formal mindfulness practice is one of the best antidotes to fixing experience into solid 'selfhood'. When we meditate, we're transforming our perspective, which can help bring a lightness to life.

Part IV

CHOICE

*'Practise not-doing, and everything
will fall into place.'*
LAO-TZU

Chapter 8

Mindful Action

*'The quality of your action depends
on the quality of your being.'*
THICH NHAT HANH

*The more we can attune in a sensory way, the more we
develop an eye, ear, nose, mind, taste and feel for the
most appropriate action to take. With space to breathe,
we may find skilful activity comes, without our having to
strain for it.*

When we buy a new piece of technology we expect it to
come with a set of instructions. Even with these in hand,
we usually accept that it may take a while to become
familiar with our purchase. We're prepared to invest time
and energy in learning how the product works because we
understand this will make it easier to use.

Yet how many of us take a similar attitude towards the
mind and body? Here we have some of the most amazing
technology in the known universe, and somehow we think
we'll pick up how it works as we go along. Of course, there
are education systems and training programmes of many

kinds, but most of these are geared towards ingesting information and performing tasks. This is like loading software onto a computer hard drive without getting a handle on the operating system.

Managing mind and body well

In mindfulness training, we focus on managing mind and body well. We become familiar with the workings of our internal processes, seeing parts and patterns with a precise, open eye. Through this process of quiet observation, we can notice what leads to wellbeing and what doesn't.

Simultaneously, we're training in working more skillfully with what we find. We gently exercise the muscle of attention by coming back when the mind wanders, and we practise staying present, neither following nor resisting impulses that lead to unhelpful action. We connect with and shift towards the experience of life

It may seem like we're not doing very much when we practise, but plenty can change in the stillness. We're performing a kind of internal alchemy. Over time, mindfulness training can open us up to a radical transformation of perspective, leading in turn to a new way of being in the world.

This sounds somewhat magical – and in some ways it is, for really we know little about this remarkable thing called consciousness. It's also in the spirit of good scientific inquiry. The subject of the study is *us*, along with our relationship to the world we live in, and we carry out the experiment from a space of awareness. With the understanding cultivated, we learn how to live more effectively.

It can be tempting to come to mindfulness training and hope for lots of techniques to help us handle specific situations. What's the right method for dealing with a parent or child, or for making the right career move, or for managing depression? Of course, there are ways to approach these situations artfully, but if we train ourselves to work with the mind and body, really getting to know how they function best, we can bring this learning to every circumstance, without needing a new set of instructions each time. Mindfulness isn't learned by filling up with information, or by forcing ourselves to be someone we're not. It comes from opening to a transformation in the *way* we experience.

Studies suggest that mindfulness can help in a wide range of educational and vocational circumstances, such as helping maintain attention and performance in the face of demanding workloads,[1] protecting professional carers from burnout and empathy drain[2], and enabling wellbeing, attention and good performance among students.[3] These highly practical benefits may partly be why mindfulness training has been introduced in many schools and universities, businesses and other organizational settings.

People experiencing many kinds of difficulties find mindfulness useful. There have been positive results from studies involving people experiencing post-traumatic stress disorder, paranoia, irritable bowel syndrome, insomnia, asthma, fibromyalgia, tinnitus, bipolar disorder, loneliness, and the stress of being a carer, among many other situations.[4] There seem to be few circumstances in which practising awareness doesn't help, and mindfulness is now an option that health professionals turn to in supporting the people they work with.

However, in each of these instances, changes seem to come as a by-product of people learning foundational practices and attitudes, such as the ones we've been exploring together, and applying what they learn to their lives. This appears to be the best way to approach the training, for as soon as we try to make mindfulness solve a particular problem, or fit a certain set of circumstances, we've already moved away from the present moment and into focusing on future results.

A problem-solving approach is sometimes counter-productive, as it can create and highlight a stressful mismatch between our current circumstance and our desired goals. Rather than trying to achieve a prescribed set of outcomes, mindfulness training helps us understand and work with the human experience itself more skillfully. If we can do that, aren't we likely to manage things better anyway?

Effortless action

This doesn't mean that action won't happen. With space to breathe, we may find skilful activity comes, but perhaps without our having to strain. Slowing down and listening to what's sometimes called 'wise mind' – the understanding that comes from connecting with mind and body – we may find ourselves drawn to make changes.

Sometimes the best action is no action (or no action yet). At other times, we may not feel ready for a particular course, even though we'd like to take it. This is okay too – we don't have to get ahead of ourselves, or try to be perfect. Sometimes we need to wait for more growth and unfolding to take place.

We may need to practise accepting what we can't change (or can't change yet), and seeing what's here in a new way. The shifts people make as they practise mindfulness are often small, but over time they can add up to greater transformations. Without having to make great plans or push for major changes, a path towards happiness and wisdom can be walked. Awareness tends to lead us into healthier circumstances, and healthier responses to those circumstances. As we experience greater contentment, we're following a virtuous, upward spiral to wellbeing.

Sustaining the virtuous spiral

This shift towards contentment can be sustained, even when things get rough. After mindfulness training, difficult emotions interfere less when people are asked to respond to events quickly – suggesting they're less likely to be knocked off a chosen course by life's challenges.[5] Along the way, we're also more likely to be compassionate to ourselves,[6] which studies suggest is a key factor in wellbeing.[7]

Whereas low mood tends to lead to more of the same, mindfulness training offers a counterweight. It's associated with increased experience and appreciation of pleasant emotions, and a greater ability to engage in activities that can increase those emotions.[8] After mindfulness training, people are more likely to remember pleasant stimuli, and this change is associated with less depression and anxiety, and a deeper sense of wellbeing.[9] They're not only more able to manage difficult experiences, but increasingly capable of appreciating and being buoyed by pleasant ones.

With mindfulness, we become more attuned to the good in our lives, and inspired towards circumstances that bring more joy. Working with the difficult and appreciating the good – these are foundations of resilience. With such qualities, we're orienting ourselves to attitudes that support and perpetuate skilful living.

Beyond stress reduction

People often find that mindfulness brings a life they hadn't expected. Perhaps they wanted to take a mindfulness course to reduce stress, and then discover that the journey goes beyond mere calming or relaxation. They find themselves engaged in an ongoing and open communion with life, recognizing the destination as unknown, and realizing contentment in the mystery, magic and delight of the journey, with all its inevitable peaks and troughs.

In mindfulness training, we put our energy into the present moment, and let this be our guide for next steps. The more we can attune in a sensory way, the more we develop an eye, ear, nose, mind, taste and feel for the most appropriate action to take. Mindfulness is associated with greater autonomy and choicefulness, as well as engagement with valued behaviours.[10]

Transformation themes – care and compassion

Because our minds, bodies and circumstances are all unique, there is no one mindful route for us all. Nevertheless, when we enter mindfulness training, a few common themes tend to emerge. Firstly, as we train in good self-care, we're usually drawn to changes that support this. This may mean looking after our bodies, such as by eating more healthily, or taking more exercise, both of which are linked to greater mindfulness.[11] Or it may mean shifting the habits of daily life: stopping smoking or watching less TV, say, or going out to meet friends more often, or taking a class to learn new skills.

We might begin a search or training for a more satisfying job, or find ourselves giving more time, money or energy to causes that inspire us. We might choose to walk when we can, rather than drive the car, perhaps taking a route that enables us to enjoy being out in nature.

We might make mental shifts in attitude, such as reminding ourselves to appreciate the large and small wonders of being alive. We might find ourselves noticing the pleasant events or interactions that occur each day. Or perhaps we might focus less on money and possessions as a way to seek happiness – it's been shown that more mindful people are less materialistic and less image and status-focused, an outlook that's associated with wellbeing.[12]

Mindfulness also trains us in compassion. As we practise being gentle to ourselves, so that attitude of mind seems naturally to expand to others. As we incline the mind to be kind (such as by acknowledging wandering and gently returning to attention), so it tends to begin offering kindness to whatever and whoever its attention falls upon.

With insight into patterns of mind and body, we can better understand the struggles of others. Deeply, we realize the shared hardships of being human, and this understanding itself can be healing, and not just for ourselves. This may be why, in a study of trainee therapists, the clients of meditators experienced a greater reduction in symptoms.[13] Similarly, employees of more mindful leaders experience greater wellbeing, as well as performing better in their jobs.[14]

Appreciating how perceptions get skewed, we understand more how conflicts arise. With the skills of clear seeing growing within us, we may become more artful in our communication and behaviour. We may realize that one of the best ways to happiness is to offer compassion to others.

This doesn't mean rolling over to unreasonable demands – indeed, sometimes the most compassionate thing we can do is to stand our ground – but can we do so with a tender heart? As our attitude of care affects those around us, aren't they more likely to trust and exhibit care for us too? Research seems to suggest that co-operative behaviours are contagious.[15] This is the road to collective wellbeing.

Experiencing the fixed, isolated self as illusion, we naturally find ourselves setting on a course to benefit the whole, rather than being out just for me and mine. We don't even need a return of generosity to experience benefits from kindness – studies have found that the act of giving money to others makes people happier than spending it on themselves.[16] An attitude of altruism is enough to bring benefits to happiness and health.[17]

We may decide more actively and explicitly to cultivate a range of mindful approaches. We might choose to practise cheerfulness, perhaps making an intention to smile more often. Smiling, it turns out, leads to quicker recovery from stressful situations, a lower heart rate and better mood, as well as heightened feelings of pleasure.[18] We may prefer not to join in with gossip, cynicism, hot-headedness or judgementalism.

We might decide to keep a gratitude diary, writing down each day the things we appreciate. This practice has been shown to improve mood, happiness and life satisfaction, and decrease symptoms of depression.[19] Or we might decide to spend more time walking in green spaces, enjoying the benefits of physical exercise and connecting with awe at the amazing world we live in – another habit that's correlated with wellbeing.[20]

We could choose to expose ourselves less to gloomy or harsh perspectives. We may decide to read or watch the news a bit less, knowing that repeated exposure to the selective, and predominantly negative, drama of the headlines will feed both unpleasant emotions and the cognitive distortions that can perpetuate them. At the same time, we may find ourselves inclined to work for change to unjust situations and systems that cause suffering. By consciously fostering practices and attitudes that lead to collective wellbeing, we're training ourselves in a wise and loving perspective, and offering it out to others.

Ethical living

This means leaning in to ethical living. Mindfulness doesn't happen in a value-free vacuum. In some traditions, meditation practice only begins after a student has spent time working on the conduct that will make it most effective.

This might include making commitments to protect life, cultivate generosity, practise good conduct in family, friend and work relationships, engage in truthful, inspiring, non-violent speech, and only partaking of non-toxic food, drink and media.[21]

Mindful ethics come not from an ideological or moral standpoint, but from the understanding that how we live affects our state of mind and body, and so the capacity for happiness and rich relationships. It's difficult, if not impossible, to develop mindfulness if we're continuing to put our energy into harmful activities. A bit of mindfulness isn't going to make much difference when our general motivation and practice is mindlessness – by continuing to train in unskilful thought and behaviour, we'll be reinforcing unhelpful habits.

We'll also likely be caught in the consequences of our actions, further heightening stress. Chances are, we won't feel so good, and neither will those around us. With an unbalanced mind and an unbalanced life, we'll be prone to poor decisions that swamp us further in difficulty.

If we can employ awareness in the service of ethical behaviour, our training can help us move mindfully in each domain of life. By tuning in to the nature and effects of our thinking, feeling and acting, and cultivating the steadfastness and space to refrain from unskilful deeds and open to and encourage wiser choices, we're freed up to notice what leads to a happy life, and given the tools to create it for ourselves and those around us.

Science seems to be showing that happiness is nurtured by actions such as taking physical exercise, committing to ongoing learning, fostering strong social connections, and practising generosity.[22] By experimenting with these approaches mindfully, and noticing what happens, we can test them in the laboratory of life.

Does how we look after our bodies and minds affect wellbeing? Do we and others feel and respond better when we're kind? When we're living, working and communicating from a compassionate perspective, does this lead to better circumstances? Does it help in our relationships?

By approaching suggestions for ethical living as invitations to be explored, rather than rules to be obeyed, we allow ourselves to tune in to and respond from a deep sense of purpose, rather than the internal slave-driver who tries to govern with 'shoulds' and 'shouldn'ts'. As well as freeing us from the tyranny of self-judgement, in which we're blamed and shamed into an imposed view of right and wrong, this gentler approach offers a greater chance of fulfilling our aspirations, because it comes from and is tested in our own experience.

Practice: The three-step breathing space, with action step

We've been practising the breathing space as a way of tuning in to the present moment and working with difficult thoughts, sensations and circumstances. It can also be explored as a first step to skilful action.

First, let's remember the three steps of the breathing space as we've been practising it so far.

Step one: Acknowledging

Adopt a confident, gentle, dignified posture, and tune in to your experience – thoughts and sensations as they're happening now. Let them be known, without having to do anything about them.

Step two: Gathering

Let go of thoughts and sensations, and bring your attention to the breath. Follow the in- and out-breath for a while.

Step three: Expanding

Opening up to a wider field, let internal and external phenomena be known in choiceless awareness. Practise just being with whatever's here, letting go of judgement and coming back to spaciousness when the attention narrows in to a smaller focus.

The action step

At this point, there are a number of choices we might explore.

Step four (a)

Having dropped into mindfulness, notice shifts in your perspective. It may be enough – or all that's possible for now – to experience from a space of awareness, with mindfulness of breathing as a way of grounding. Or you can practise a more open awareness, noticing thoughts as just thoughts, sensations as just sensations, and circumstances as part of the ever-changing flow of life events.

You could remind yourself that 'this too shall pass'. Perhaps no further action is required? If stress or difficulty has arisen, you could practise moving towards it, connecting courageously and compassionately with sensations and thoughts as they appear in the moment, reminding yourself that it's okay to let them arise, be known, and pass through in kindly awareness.

Step four (b)

As we tune in to our situation with the breathing space, it may seem that mindful action is required. Checking that the choice to 'do' comes from the space of discerning awareness, rather than a reactive habit, you could heartfully inquire: 'How can I best take care of things right now? What would be a wise and compassionate response to this situation?' Allow yourself to see the whole picture of the situation – your own perspective and also that of any others involved.

Listen to answers that arise from within. If any seem practical and sensible to follow through, explore them from a place of conscious presence. Be willing to change or stay the course, taking into account the ongoing internal and external feedback you receive. If no clear answers come, respect the space of 'no answers yet', waiting with patience for a more auspicious time.

Step four (c)

Without denying the difficult, trying to force positivity, or pushing for pleasure that isn't available, allow yourself to open to and drink in enjoyable sights, sounds, feelings, tastes and smells. Evidence suggests that holding emotionally stimulating experiences in awareness leads to increases in neural activity and stronger memory traces of the event.[1]

By more consciously appreciating pleasant events as they appear, and turning our attention towards what we find nurturing, we may be flavouring our implicit memories – tilting our perspective towards contentment – and calibrating away from negativity bias.

Can you appreciate having food to eat, air to breathe, a body and mind to experience with? Can you appreciate this moment of being alive? The act of appreciating itself may generate feelings of wellbeing.

Step four (d)

Experiment with actions that are known to be helpful – taking exercise, meeting friends, connecting with nature, or writing a gratitude list. Ask yourself: what might be the most ethical response to this situation?

Remember to consider care for yourself and others in your contemplation. What action, if any, best expresses your deepest values? Listen to your wise mind and body, remembering that sometimes the most skilful response is to do nothing, or stay present and wait for inspiration to occur.

Training in kindness

Compassion is implicit in every moment of mindfulness. By returning to awareness gently when we notice the mind has wandered, bringing a warm-hearted acceptance to thoughts and sensations, we're strengthening our capacity for kindness.

Just like attention itself, the attitude with which we attend is trainable. By explicitly cultivating compassion, we're opening the gift of benevolence, which lets us live life with loving eyes. Our interpretations of events may become softer and more generous. Further opening to a sense of connection, we're perhaps more able to feel and appreciate our own and others' difficulties (without being overwhelmed by them), relating with empathy and understanding.

By experiencing situations with kindness, we feel less resistant to or irritated by them. By offering compassion to others, we're reducing the likelihood of interpersonal conflict, allowing a warm space in which people can heal and thrive. It's more likely in this space that others will find it in themselves to be kind, although we can't rely on this to happen. If we need to take decisions that others won't like, we can allow these to come from a place of deep mutual interest.

Practising kindness is strongly linked to wellbeing. Programmes that train compassion through meditation are associated with increases in emotions such as awe and gratitude,[23] reduced depressive symptoms and greater life satisfaction,[24] as well as greater connectedness with others.

In tests of generosity, participants trained in compassion are more likely to help those in need.[25] They become less upset when exposed to stressful situations and have reduced levels of interleukin-6, a chemical implicated in both stress and a range of major health conditions such as heart disease, diabetes and some cancers.[26]

Practice: Loving-kindness meditation

Here are some guidelines for cultivating compassion through a practice called loving-kindness meditation, which is often taught alongside mindfulness. Loving-kindness practice explicitly cultivates the compassion that's implied in all mindfulness training.

1. Take a dignified posture as previously described, and practise mindfulness of breathing for a while. Allow some time and space for dropping into 'being'.

2. Bring to mind someone who has been kind to you, and for whom you feel gratitude. Visualizing them in front of you, recall the ways

they've helped you. Let any feelings be experienced in your body (without trying to force them).

Seeing the goodness in this person, say to them mentally: *May you be safe, may you be free from suffering, may you experience peace.* Use other phrases if they feel more true for you – the words aren't as important as the sentiment you offer. (Other possibilities include: *May you enjoy wellbeing, may you be free from harm, may you be happy, may you be healthy,* or *may you be released from stress.*)

Let the words come, as best you can, from your whole being, rather than just from the thinking mind. Feel their energy within you. If you like, imagine giving the person a hug as you send them good wishes. It doesn't matter if what you're doing feels awkward or inauthentic – treat this as an experiment and remember, whatever comes up is okay.

3. When you feel ready, let the image of the benefactor fade, and bring to mind a friend or family member for whom you feel love. It's a good idea to choose someone for whom your love is uncomplicated and heartfelt, rather than tinged with desire or resentment.

    Offer this person your good wishes too, gently repeating the same or similar phrases as before. You might like to imagine embracing the loved one. Let whatever feelings come up be experienced. If at any point during the practice you feel overwhelmed, it's okay to drop the visualization and return to mindfulness of breathing or stop. Explore the practice gently.

4. Now imagine that it's you appearing in your mind's eye. Experiment with offering yourself the same sense of loving-kindness, as a person worthy of compassion and care. Open to this sense of warm-heartedness towards your own being. Repeat the same or similar phrases silently to yourself: *May I be happy, may I be healthy, may I be at peace.* If you experience resistance, notice and be interested in this, as best you can without buying into opinions about it.

You might like to recall kind or generous things that you've done in the past, or qualities about yourself that you like. If none come up, or you feel guilt or disappointment or another difficult emotion, know this is not a failure or a problem – experiment with observing without attachment, returning perhaps to mindfulness of body for a time. When the mind wanders away, acknowledge this gently and return to the visualization, or the phrases, or the feeling of what's happening.

5. Now call to mind someone for whom your feelings are generally neutral. Perhaps someone who you don't know so well – such as an acquaintance you see occasionally, but for whom there's no strong liking or disliking. See that this person too is a human being, vulnerable to the stresses of life. Like everyone, they want to be happy, and like everyone, they sometimes make mistakes. Practise wishing them happiness, health and safety as they journey through existence.

6. If you feel able, now bring to mind someone with whom you have difficulty. Perhaps not choosing (to begin with) a person for whom your dislike or anger is very strong, but someone you experience as perhaps challenging or irritating, or with whom you are in some conflict.

Open to the reality that this person is human as well, and wants to be happy – perhaps they're doing the best they can in their circumstances. You might consider their positive qualities, recognizing what they're good at. Perhaps they're suffering as a result of their behaviour – contemplating this may open the window of compassion.

Letting go of judgements as best you can, practise offering this person loving-kindness too, wishing them well in their lives. Remember that offering kindness doesn't mean you're condoning any unskilful behaviour or harm done. Whatever feelings come, let these be as they are – there's no wrong way to be feeling as you practise this.

If this feels or becomes too difficult, it's completely okay to return to mindfulness of breathing or to sending loving-kindness to the benefactor, friend or ourselves once more. We could also choose to practise loving-kindness for aspects of ourselves that we find difficult, or tend to deny.

7. Finally, picturing all the people you have visualized together, including yourself, offer a sense of kindness and warmth to the whole group – saying to yourself something like: *May we all be safe, may we all be free from stress, may we all experience peace*.

If you like, you could extend your compassion out further – to the whole town you live in, or even to all beings on the planet. Visualize the energy of kindness radiating out from your heart, extending far and wide.

Intention is key here, rather than result, so it's not a problem if you don't feel loving-kindness during or after this meditation. Just keep working with the practice as best you can, noticing what comes up and bringing a friendly acceptance to this too, as best you can.

Week 8: practices to explore

- Train with any combination of the practices we've been exploring so far. This could be mindfulness of breath, body, sounds, thoughts, and choiceless awareness or the five senses practice, along with the three-step breathing space.

- Practise for as long each day as feels manageable for you. Explore working with a schedule you think you could continue for the next phase of your life. For now, just see how it goes this week, and at the end reflect back and make any changes that seem wise.

- Practise the breathing space with the action step. Experiment with it especially when you need to make a decision, or when you feel stressed and impelled to act. See if you can allow any actions to come from your whole being: mind and body together, moment by moment. Notice what happens, and also when and how you feel fragmented. Be interested in the connections between what you do, think and feel.

- Write down a list of everything you've done today (or yesterday). Be as complete as you can. Looking at the list, notice whether you found each activity 'nourishing' or 'depleting', bringing awareness to how you feel as your eyes read what you've written. Did an activity lead you to feel more inspired, uplifted and energized, or more deflated, tired or flat? If you felt nourished by an activity, write an N next to it, and if you felt depleted, write a D next to it.

  Now ask yourself: is there one thing you could do to shift the balance towards more nourishment? Be realistic, recognizing that most of us have responsibilities that mean doing some things we don't like or don't find easy. Can you make an intention for just one small change? Doing more of something, less of something, or trying something new?

  See if you can let inspiration for change come from the whole body, rather than following an idea of something you 'should' or 'shouldn't' do'. Does this plan fit with your values? Is it practical? Is it gentle and kind?

Experiment with making this small change, and then after one week repeat the writing exercise. What effect did the change have? Is it something you could continue? Perhaps you'd like to explore a different small shift? This is something that can be done again and again, each time offering information on how we're feeling about our actions, leading us into gentle, authentic, forward steps. This can be a more effective way to make shifts than trying to make single great leaps, which may be unrealistic and unsustainable.

- Experiment with the loving-kindness meditation a few times this week. Notice and be interested in what comes up when you practise.
- Choose a C of mindfulness to work with this week, following the guidance in chapter 2.

Simon's experience

Work and how I responded to it used to be one of my biggest triggers, and that has really transformed. A colleague said to me: 'You seem very different in meetings, much quieter.' I guess I was quite loud and opinionated, almost by default taking up a position of being 'against' everything. I don't do that anymore, as I don't think that's the best way to move forward and get things done. It doesn't feel right to react by shouting and stamping my feet.

My ambition now is to have more free time, more quiet time. I've even gone to my major clients and said: 'I'm going to have to put a cut-off point on how much time I can give you because I've got other things I want to do.' And those other things are taking the dog for a walk and meditating – quiet things. That's so different from a little while ago. It's a real re-alignment.

I've become aware that in every situation, you have the opportunity to express kindness, compassion and gratitude, and wherever possible I like to take it. There's a selfish side to it because I feel good when I do that, and it also seems to make everybody else feel good as well. It just seems to be a much happier way of being. I can take the dog for a walk and maybe have some really nice interactions with a few people, maybe do somebody a favour or compliment them. I don't have to wait till August every year to be happy.

Ann's experience

There was a missing link for me between being aware and doing something about it, and mindfulness has filled that gap. I can ask myself: 'What are the consequences of a decision – what could happen?' and 'Which would be the best route?' I never made time for that before because I felt like I couldn't get off that treadmill or I'd be upsetting too many people. Now I'm not in a rush. I have a habit of taking time out.

My instinct for life going forward is to make it a lot simpler – it doesn't need to be complicated. That doesn't mean I'll just sit in an armchair knitting, but it

does mean I don't need to do everything. I don't need
to be the best, I don't need to put pressure on myself
to worry what other people think.

Andy's experience

These days I work as a psychologist. I try to help
people make sense of their experience, and with what
they do or don't do with it. Mindfulness has led to a
huge shift in my work – I now practise psychology
differently. It's more process-driven, helping people
understand why they get stuck in patterns, rather than
just the content of what's happening.

In healthcare, mindfulness could have a huge impact,
such as on the lives of people with long-term
conditions. And there'd probably be a knock-on
effect, because people wouldn't be turning up in the
emergency room at hospital every time they're having
a twinge – when they think they're having a heart
attack and they're probably just feeling anxious.

If more people meditated, there might be less
kneejerk anger, less envy and greed. Meditation
helps people be more confident, more happy in their
own being, which will lead to better relationships
with others. If you're insensitive to other people, it's
probably because you're not listening to your own
messages about what's going on.

Catherine's experience

Meditating changes the way I think and act – the way I respond to things. I'm able to pause, be patient, and have that self-control I always wished for. If there's a big argument or an issue with the kids I deal with it better – I've more resilience. It's in split seconds but I'm able to suddenly notice they're upset about something so I don't need to tell them off about it. It's okay if I'm irritated – I don't need to take it out on them.

I act with more authenticity because I'm more in tune with myself. I instinctively do the things that matter to me, without thinking about it that much. I can feel my way, rather than thinking. I'm in my head a lot, so it's quite good to have another form of guidance – from my inner self, my intuition, my body. There's a flow between mind and body so they're working together, and things happen more easily.

A lot of people think they've no choice – if they feel a certain way or they respond in a certain way they think it's not their responsibility. It's really useful to teach people that you can actually choose how you're going to respond. You can be aware. It's a practice thing – the more you do it, the more you get into the habit of doing it, even if it feels fake at first.

SUMMARY

- Letting ourselves trust in the space of awareness, we may find ourselves opening to a bigger picture, and less caught in reactivity. As we experience greater contentment, and express that through our behaviour, we're following a sustainable, upward spiral to wellbeing.

- Awareness of the workings of mind and body naturally draws us into situations conducive to wellbeing. Mindfulness is associated with greater autonomy and choicefulness – along with authenticity and coherence – as well as engagement with valued behaviours.

- Understanding mind and body brings insight into the lives of others, igniting a compassion for their struggles. Compassion is implicit in every moment of mindfulness, and by explicitly cultivating this through loving-kindness meditation, we're opening the gift of benevolence. This helps us live life with loving eyes.

- Practising kindness is strongly linked to wellbeing.

- The ethics of mindfulness come from understanding that how we live our lives affects wellbeing. The breathing space can be explored as a first step to mindful action.

Chapter 9

Wholeness

'(Mindfulness is) the unfailing master key for knowing the mind and is thus the starting point, the perfect tool for shaping the mind and is thus the focal point (and)... the lofty manifestation of the achieved freedom of the mind and is thus the culmination point.'

NYANAPONIKA THERA

Understanding, sustaining and acting from a mindful perspective is likely to be a lifelong training, requiring our ongoing, gentle effort. We can let go of getting to perfect mindfulness, and instead work simply on bringing awareness to our lives, moment by moment. Whenever we remember to live from awareness, we're practising mindfulness.

Mindfulness is not just a set of techniques. Seeing patterns of mind and body in communion with circumstance, we're offered the gift of awareness. Learning the capacity to stay present to an ever-changing flow of inner and outer experience, we find freedom from reactivity and the possibility of wiser, more conscious action.

Practising attitudes conducive to wellbeing, we uncover a wholesome perspective that dissolves the painful defences of imagined 'selfhood', easing our path through the world. This enables greater enjoyment of pleasant events, a deepened capacity to negotiate hardships, and a finer-tuned skill in relating to connected others with confidence and compassion.

Put simply, mindfulness is an ABC skill: we cultivate Awareness by Being with experience, and this leads to Choice.

As we've discovered, mindfulness is trainable. Through the gentle, repeating work of meditation, we're shown our current circumstances and given the know-how to gradually transform our relationship to them. By cultivating this shift, we invoke the possibility of creative, compassionate action, and this can become a foundation for skilful doing, or non-doing, as appropriate. Wise decision-making nurtures an ethical, values-inspired lifestyle that allows for expansion of the peace we may be starting to glimpse more often.

Embodied learning

As an experiential practice rather than a theory, ideology or set of concepts, mindfulness means bringing awareness to present-moment phenomena (thoughts and sensations) as they appear in mind and body, observing, attuning and responding to these events, perhaps in a new way. This requires a willingness to experiment, exploring the suggestions of practitioners past.

We don't have to buy in to dogma: if a shift in view occurs, it emerges from our own experience, rather than a mere change in belief. This enables our learning to be embodied.

By opening to seeing, feeling, hearing, tasting, smelling – we can develop deftness in our minds, hearts and life. This is the font of wellbeing, and of astute, sensitive action.

Buddhism, the contemplative tradition with which mindfulness practice is most closely associated, has sometimes been described as 'a science of mind'. Emphasis is placed on testing out the hypotheses put forward by its teachers – is our inner and outer world as described, and does working with it as prescribed lead to contentment? Willing to follow a set of methods, the practitioner notices what happens and learns from what's realized. Awareness is the scientific observer that watches and reflects on the flow of events in the internal and external world.

A union of art and science

Quantitative methods have brought a new kind of rigour to this ancient way. Many researchers engaged in this work are also mindfulness practitioners, able to use their first-person experience to guide the design of studies which can give a more objective view. These contemplative scientists are producing empirical data that demonstrates with precision when and how mindfulness is helpful. There is, as always, much to discover, but an alliance of ancient and modern approaches has already led to new understandings of how wellbeing can be found and maintained.

The Dalai Lama once said that while Western scientists were exploring outer space, great meditators in the East were exploring inner space. Bringing the learning from both kinds of inquiry together, using the technology of awareness and of MRI scanners, EEG machines and data analysis, we may find ever more fruitful means of accessing the freedom and peace that great teachers through the ages have said is possible.

Into wholeness

As we enter a path of mindfulness – purposefully, attentively, and gently – we let go into a journey that naturally and gradually inclines to wholeness. Tuning in to feedback from mind, body and environment, we learn to trust in meditative tools, realizing that they're usually enough to guide us, so long as we learn to use them well.

Just as attention wanders when we practise meditation, so we'll likely revert to painful old habits again and again, but rather than upbraiding ourselves, we can choose to see this as part of the dance of life. Off the hook of having to get it all together, we're free to enjoy the journey as it happens.

Dropping the need for a certain result – even an experience of wellbeing – might seem difficult at first, entailing as it does a relinquishing of control. But if we're willing to accept uncertainty, we may discover that wellbeing finds us without our having to strain for it. A wellbeing that can be experienced without conditions – isn't this happiness indeed?

A mindful world?

When each of us commits to the path of mindfulness, a pivotal point is reached in our life. Going against the stream of automaticity, we're starting to face our predicament squarely, and to live our lives more consciously.

As our practice deepens, we may come to influence others to take a similar step – it's often said that mindfulness is 'caught', as much as it's 'taught'. If enough people are inspired to live in this way, the possibilities for influencing the world in the direction of wisdom and compassion are great, especially in this time of complex political, social and environmental challenge.

How this might unfold is speculation, but it's encouraging that moves are being made to mindfulness not just in healthcare but in education, business, politics, the law, digital media and the arts, as well as many other arenas where people meet, connect and communicate. Mindfulness has been taught in settings ranging from Google headquarters in California to the English Houses of Parliament, as well as in a great number of schools, clinics, social service organizations, workplaces, retreat centres and festivals, as well as online.

We don't need to try too hard. The way of mindfulness is as much of an undoing as a doing, especially for those of us bent on achievement. It seems that when we give up our habits of clinging, craving and avoidance, a wise, compassionate, skilful awareness can arise in the space, without our having to strain for it.

Practice: Mindful Movement (Walking)

Meditation doesn't have to be practised in stillness. Any movement can be mindful, as we bring awareness to it. Mindfulness while moving can be practised with traditional forms such as yoga or tai chi, or by bringing awareness to activities such as swimming, running, cycling, cooking, cleaning the house and washing the dishes. By noticing sensations and thoughts, we can discover new ways of experiencing activities that we regularly engage in.

We might find, for example, that washing the dishes becomes a more interesting experience when we connect with the sensations of soap and water on the hands, watching the judgements that tell us it's unpleasant or boring. Or perhaps we might become more aware of the slave-driver in us as we exercise, learning to let go of pushing and pulling ourselves too far and too fast.

Many of us are in movement much of the time, and by remembering to tune in to body sensations as we travel, we're reminding ourselves to be present in daily life.

One simple and traditional way of moving mindfully is walking meditation, described below. As a practice that invites a sense of groundedness, it can be good to practise this especially when we feel fragmented, anxious or spaced out.

1. Find a place where you can safely and comfortably walk – this can be indoors, in any room where you can move from one end to the other, or outside, say in a garden or park. Depending on where you're walking, you might like to try this without shoes. Make an intention for how long you'll practise.

2. Stand, perhaps opening your awareness to the whole body for a time, or taking some moments to scan the body from toes to head.

3. Direct your attention to sensations in the soles of the feet. Feel the feet on the floor – the connection of body to Earth.

4. Begin to take a step, lifting one foot off the floor slowly, being interested in which foot, and which part of that foot, you find yourself raising first. Notice other parts of the leg moving too.

Feel your weight shifting forwards as you come into the downward movement, the foot coming back towards the floor.

Bring awareness to the moment of contact, and the recalibration of the body with each aspect of the movement. Now step with the other foot (has this step already begun, without your being aware of it?).

5. Continue to walk, gently bringing the mind back to sensations in the feet when you notice it wandering away. Notice any tendencies to want to speed up, or to try to get somewhere. Notice how it is to be walking without a goal or destination. If you're walking inside, and reach one end of the room, make a turn and continue to walk back to the other end.

6. As best you can, let there be a sense of confidence, lightness and precision to your walking, without forcing. Be interested in what happens – are you noticing any habitual patterns (rushing, zoning out, tensing)? Observe and let go with kindness. Continue walking like this for as long as you've intended.

Possible variations to explore:

-   As well as practising mindful walking with attention in the feet, try it with a wider acknowledgement of sensations in the whole body.

-   Expanding further, you could also include the full sensory palette in your practice – noticing sights, sounds and smells, or giving some attention to each at different times.

-   Making this a more informal practice, try mindful walking at 'regular' pace. Do you notice when you've missed moments in rumination or distraction? Slow down and come back to focus in the feet, as a means of grounding attention.

Continuing your practice

Automatic patterns of distraction and reacting are persistent, and so the path of mindfulness continues. There are a number of tried and tested ways of helping this to happen.

Sustaining formal meditation

It's good to carve out a regular time and space for ongoing meditation practice. By committing to this on a daily basis, we're reminding ourselves of the value we place on awareness, and training ourselves in it. Like any skill, the more we practise, the more we're likely to be able to manifest it spontaneously.

Make an intention for the practices you'd like to follow, how often and for how long. You could make a schedule for a period of a month, say, to begin with. Like an athlete preparing for a marathon, stick to what you've decided, whatever the internal and external weather. Re-set the intention (it can be good to write it down) at the end of the time period you've agreed with yourself, using what you've learned to make any appropriate adjustments (e.g. to the amount of time you devote to it, the time of day to practise, etc).

Mindfulness courses

It can be very nurturing to practise mindfulness with others, especially when guided by an experienced teacher. There are a number of good mindfulness courses (many of them following the model of eight weekly sessions) that offer training in the foundations of mindfulness. For those unable to find a local group, there are some courses available online. Practising intensively on a retreat (anything from a day to a month or more in duration) can also be transformative. There are some further resources at the end of this book to help you find a course or retreat.

Reading and study

Understanding the framework for mindfulness (its rationale, history, and attitudinal foundations) is a strong support for practice, although not an adequate substitute for it. Hearing how other people are working with mindfulness in their lives can also be a good reminder and inspiration. As well as books, there are magazines, websites, blogs, audios and videos that can offer support. There's more information on how to access these in the further resources section.

Informal mindfulness practice

We're practising mindfulness whenever we remember to live from awareness. As we've discovered, this is more easily said than done, and so the time and space for formal meditation continues to offer a foundation for this work. However, we can also extend our practice to any situation, using life events themselves as an opportunity to return to presence. Here are a few suggestions for how you might practise everyday mindfulness:

- Place some coloured stickers around the house, as visual reminders to stop and feel the breath and/or body. You might decide to take a moment's mindful pause before you open the front door, answer the phone, get out of bed, or turn on the computer.

- Use waiting times as an opportunity to tune in to your mind, body and environment. Feel your feet on the ground and breathe (perhaps silently saying to yourself: two feet, one breath), noticing any sensations or thoughts that arise. Perhaps there's an internal tightness or pressure, and thoughts of wanting to move faster. Could the experience of being 'stuck' in a queue or traffic jam be welcomed as a chance to be present and still? Might this transform the experience of being delayed?

- Practise during routine activities. Mindful eating, driving, exercise and cleaning all become possible by being willing to experience with a friendly interest. Notice when you get caught in attempted multi-tasking: can you allow yourself to practise one activity at a time? What changes, if anything, when you do this?

- Explore bringing mindfulness to your relationship with others. What happens when you listen, speak and act from a place of centredness? Or when you relate from a more fractured or distracted mind?

Practice: STOP – a one-minute mindfulness practice

This simple and easy-to-remember practice takes a minute or so, offering an opportunity to shift into mindfulness at any point.

1. **S**TOP whatever you're doing (provided it's safe to do so). Let go into being.

2. **T**ake a few mindful breaths.

3. **O**pen your attention to the body, and **O**bserve the experience. What's going on with you right now? Stay present and see for some moments.

4. **P**roceed with activity. Experiment with approaching it from a more mindful perspective.

Week 9: practices to explore

- Using any combination of the practices in this book, make a plan for how you'd like to engage with mindfulness over the next month. What you choose to do will depend on your schedule and motivation – be bold and realistic. Be interested in what happens as you carry out your plan. Set a date for re-evaluating the schedule.

- Explore the further resources section in this book. What supports could you enlist for yourself? Could you commit to joining a mindfulness group, or checking in with mindful social media, or continuing your reading? Bring awareness to any tendency for reading to squeeze out the practice itself.

- Consider what obstacles get in the way of mindfulness for you. These might include buying into busyness, anxiety, boredom, resistance or frustration. Do you experience 'practice-interfering thoughts' (the PITs) such as doubt about the value of meditation, or about whether you can sustain it, or perhaps that you don't deserve the time or space, or that you can't be bothered? Write down a list of your obstacles to mindfulness, together with some reminders of approaches and activities that help you stay connected. Pin it in a place where you can see it every day.

- Write yourself a letter gently reminding yourself how you might think or feel in a time of stress or low mood.

Suggest some nurturing activities that might help, or offer words of support. Seal it up and mark it for opening at a later date, when you feel in need of inspiration.

- Choose a C of mindfulness to work with this week, following the guidance in chapter 2.

Simon's experience

Meditation practice keeps me in tune with my insides. I might have learned how to ride the 'mindfulness bike' but now I've got to keep my body fit and the machine oiled. It requires a bit of effort, but is it really an effort to 'be' for a while?

Mindfulness has helped with turning around my perspective. I'm 52 now and someone said to me the other day: 'What's it like being 52?' I said: 'The last two and a half years have been the happiest of my life.' Looking at external circumstances, you wouldn't say that those years have been massively different, but the way I've been perceiving them has been.

Ann's experience

Mindfulness is a lifetime's work. Doing the course and practising has been a huge support and a tool to make changes. I feel it's acted as a kind of conduit – it's helped me to stop enabling other people and start enabling me. There's been a shift – I've changed my relationship with myself.

Usually I do my practice at night using headphones – it helps me to sleep. I've got a few books and CDs and a mindfulness app. I have a variety so I can dip in and out of them. I don't need that formal guidance so much now, as it's much more of a habit, but I still go back to the audios to reinforce it, or I might read something.

It's very subtle – by practising you realize you've started doing things more consciously. It doesn't feel like I'm on a treadmill anymore. I've got some choices and control over what I do, more than before I started. I still have a few habits, but I recognize when I'm perpetuating them.

Andy's experience

I think mindfulness has made me stronger and more robust emotionally. It seems to nourish me, bringing a certain kind of discipline to my life. It calms my anxiety, and I feel lighter in spirit and better able to relate to other people, because I'm not so caught up in myself. These days I'm able to be with myself. It's not doing anything hugely different from an outside perspective, but it feels very powerful on the inside. I'm glad I've got it in my toolbox.

I do a lot of mini-practices most days, like the breathing space. I use it in between seeing patients, to reset and ground myself, because my work as a psychologist can be quite hard. At the beginning I used CDs of the body scan but I tend to just sit in silence now and focus on the breath for 20 or 30 minutes. I also try to practise mindful swimming every other day, focusing on the breath; I like mindful walking too. We might say that we haven't got time to fit it in, but how much time do we spend on Facebook, or in the pub?

Life throws us curveballs but most of it is what we're doing to ourselves. Being able to understand that is a huge thing. If there are two key messages from mindfulness, one is being kind to yourself and the other is that it doesn't always have to be this way. I spent most of my twenties and thirties not being very kind to myself, and I certainly wasn't wise. I'm working on the wisdom and the kindness is getting easier.

Catherine's experience

I'm in a far better place now than at the beginning of the course. I'm much kinder to myself, and I don't judge every single action. Mindfulness has been really good for me. At the same time it's been difficult because it's a habit that you need to put in your life – sometimes it's hard to do that when you have young kids.

I go to follow-up practice sessions, which are really good because they've kept me connected. At home I used to listen to guided meditations but recently I've just sat down on my cushion and done it for myself – just noticing and feeling. I might practise mindfulness of sounds or breath or body, or do a loving-kindness meditation.

My husband says mindfulness has really changed me – I can deal with things better now. I'm calmer and able to react more authentically. I'm looking after myself in other ways too – improving my diet and taking physical exercise. Meditation and being mindful is a foundation for feeling good, alive, and for having energy.

I feel like it's changed my life – I've been learning and reading about psychology and self-help for over a decade and a lot has helped, but mindfulness has been the thing that's changed everything. I'm convinced I'll be doing it in some form forever, because it's been so useful.

SUMMARY

- With practice, we can realize habits of happiness, sustainable through the ups and downs of living.

- As we enter onto a path of mindfulness – purposefully, attentively, and gently – we let go into a journey that naturally leads towards wellbeing.

- There's no need to try and improve ourselves – rather, we can let go into the mystery of who we are.

- Meditation doesn't have to be practised in stillness. Any movement can be mindful, if we bring awareness to it.

- Automatic patterns of distraction and reacting are persistent. We can let go of getting to perfect mindfulness and instead work simply on bringing awareness to our lives through formal and informal practice.

- Continuing to carve out a regular time and space for meditation seems to be important. We can also extend our practice to any situation, using life events themselves as an opportunity to be present.

Recommended Reading

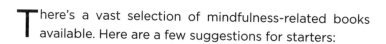

There's a vast selection of mindfulness-related books available. Here are a few suggestions for starters:

When Things Fall Apart: Heart Advice for Difficult Times, Pema Chödrön (Shambhala Publications, 1997)
I would recommend any and all of Pema Chödrön's books, which present meditation from a Buddhist perspective in a way that's accessible for all.

Full Catastrophe Living: How to Cope with Stress, Pain and Illness Using Mindfulness Meditation, Jon Kabat-Zinn (Piatkus, 2013)
Jon Kabat-Zinn developed the Mindfulness-Based Stress Reduction (MBSR) course and is the pioneer in bringing mindfulness to mainstream settings. This book sets out the MBSR programme in depth. I would also highly recommend his *Wherever You Go, There You Are: Mindfulness Meditation in Everyday Life* (Hyperion, 1994) and the accompanying audio CDs to his books, which are available from www.mindfulnesscds.com

A Path with Heart: A Guide Through the Perils and Promises of Spiritual Life, Jack Kornfield (Bantam, 1993)

Jack Kornfield has devoted his life to bringing Eastern wisdom to the West and presenting it in an accessible form. I would recommend any of his books.

Mindfulness: A Practical Guide to Finding Peace in a Frantic World, Mark Williams, Danny Penman (Piatkus, 2011)
Mark Williams is one of the developers of the MBCT course, and here he sets it out for a general audience. Comes with a practice CD led by Mark.

The Mindful Manifesto: How Doing Less and Noticing More Can Help Us Thrive in a Stressed-Out World, Jonty Heaversedge, Ed Halliwell (Hay House, 2012)
Sets out the case for mindfulness as a vital practice for the 21st century.

Search Inside Yourself: The Unexpected Path to Achieving Success, Happiness (and World Peace), Chade Meng Tan (HarperCollins, 2013)
A lively and straight-talking coursebook for the workplace mindfulness programme developed at Google.

Minding Closely: The Four Applications of Mindfulness, B. Alan Wallace (Snow Lion, 2011)
An insightful exploration of mindfulness from a Buddhist perspective, written by a foremost scholar, practitioner and scientist.

Further Resources

'Enlightenment is an accident, but meditation practice makes you accident-prone.'

ZEN SAYINGS

There's only so much mindfulness you can learn from a book, or on your own. It's a bit like reading about playing the piano – interesting, perhaps, but you probably won't develop your skills much. Without a teacher to guide you, and others to play alongside, the learning will be somewhat theoretical. Fortunately, there are a rapidly increasing number of ways that you can connect with mindfulness teachers and communities. Below are a few suggestions for developing your practice further.

Mindfulness courses

A gold standard mindfulness course is the eight-week Mindfulness-Based Stress Reduction (MBSR) programme developed by Jon Kabat-Zinn at the University of Massachussetts in the USA. It has been taught for over 35 years, and courses can be found all over the world. In the UK, a directory of MBSR courses can be found on the Be Mindful website (www.bemindful.co.uk), and you can also search for local providers.

Do check out the background and training of the person teaching – there's currently no accreditation for mindfulness teachers, but there is a set of good practice guidelines for them to follow. You can find these at www.mindfulnessteachersuk.org.uk/pdf/teacher-guidelines.pdf.

There are a number of mindfulness courses based on MBSR. The best known of these is mindfulness-based cognitive therapy (MBCT), although there are many others (mindfulness-based relapse prevention (MBRP), mindfulness-based relationship enhancement (MBRE), and so on). These take the MBSR course structure as their core, and make minor adaptations for particular circumstances. If in doubt, an MBSR course is a good starting point, as it's suitable for most people in most circumstances.

It may also be helpful to attend introductory sessions or workshops, both to get a sense of what a course involves and a feel for how a teacher works. If you're inspired by the Buddhist tradition, there are many courses run by Buddhist organizations which present mindfulness in this traditional context.

I lead mindfulness courses and workshops in the English county of Sussex and in London (see www.mindfulnesssussex.co.uk and www.mindfulnesslondon.co.uk for more details). At Mindfulness Sussex, we also offer practice sessions for people who've completed a course. I also run bespoke mindfulness courses for organizations – see www.workwithmindfulness.com if you're interested in offering a course in your workplace.

Mindfulness retreats

It's also possible to learn mindfulness in a residential retreat setting, allowing time and space to deepen your practice. These can range in length from one day to a month, or longer. I run introductory weekend retreats in the UK, as well as retreats for people who've already completed an eight-week mindfulness course – see www.mindfulnessretreats. co.uk for more details.

You might also like to look at the retreats run by the Centre For Mindfulness Research and Practice at Bangor University (www.bangor.ac.uk/mindfulness/) in Wales, and Gaia House (www.gaiahouse.co.uk), which is a UK Buddhist retreat centre offering a wide range of mindfulness-related programmes.

Mindfulness online

Where possible, I'd recommend learning mindfulness face-to-face, in a group, with an experienced teacher. However, sometimes this isn't possible, and there are resources available for people who can't get to a group, or as an additional support. Here are a few pointers:

www.bemindfulonline.com

A four-week introductory mindfulness course hosted by the Mental Health Foundation. Includes audio downloads, video guidance and email reminders. It's taught by my colleague Tessa Watt and I.

www.mindful.org

Online content from the team behind *Mindful* magazine. News, features, practice guidance and blogs, including my regular blog 'The Examined Life'.

Twitter

It's easy to connect to the mindfulness and meditation world through some key Twitter accounts. Good starting points are @mindfulonline, @greatergoodsc, @_wildmind, @mindfuleveryday and @shambhalasun. I tweet from @edhalliwell and post mindfulness news, quotes, poems and other links most days.

www.edhalliwell.com

If you're interested in exploring more of my mindfulness work and writing, there's lots of information and links here.

Acknowledgements

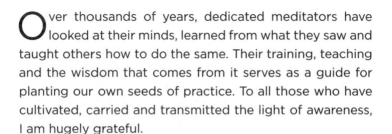

Over thousands of years, dedicated meditators have looked at their minds, learned from what they saw and taught others how to do the same. Their training, teaching and the wisdom that comes from it serves as a guide for planting our own seeds of practice. To all those who have cultivated, carried and transmitted the light of awareness, I am hugely grateful.

In recent decades, a number of pioneering practitioners have surveyed the western terrain and had the insight to present this meditative wisdom in forms and language that speak to and meet our culture's needs. Without trailblazing teachers like Jon Kabat-Zinn, and the many scientists who have spent painstaking years observing and reporting the effects of meditation on the human mind, brain and body, mindfulness might still be seen as something esoteric and weird, rather than (as is becoming more common) widely relevant and normal. A heartfelt bow to all of you.

In my own training, I have been blessed with a number of wise and kind teachers. Great gratitude goes especially to Sakyong Mipham Rinpoche and everyone in the Shambhala community, with whom I first learned to practise meditation.

More recently, I am also indebted to the community of mindfulness teachers, in particular my patient and precise supervisor Karunavira and the other team members at the Mindfulness Centre For Research and Practice at Bangor University. From afar, I have also learned a lot from Chogyam Trungpa Rinpoche, Jack Kornfield, Pema Chödrön, Alan B. Wallace, Ken Wilber, Larry Rosenberg, Bodhipaksa and Rick Hanson.

I'm also deeply grateful to the participants on mindfulness courses, retreats and workshops I've led. Their willingness to engage with and share their experience is what makes teaching such a joy – reminding me when I forget that every moment is interesting, refreshing, different and alive. Thank you as well to all the places and organizations that offer space in which our courses can happen, especially the Old School in Cuckfield, West Sussex; The School of Life in London and Claridge House in Surrey. Thanks especially to the Old School and its youth club, which generously offered me a room in which to write this book.

Thanks too to Steph Ebdon, my agent, and Carolyn Thorne, my commissioning editor, who have cajoled and nurtured me through the process of becoming an author, as well as to the team at Hay House UK, who have helped make this book happen. Special thanks to my copy editor Debra Wolter, who made skilful cuts without causing unnecessary pain.

There are many, many other people who have contributed to the contents of this book than I have space to thank – my apologies for not being able to mention you all.

However, I must acknowledge that this book wouldn't be possible without the support of my family. In more ways than I have words to describe, my wife Vicki has worked tirelessly and selflessly to make it possible for me to write and run courses – everything from coming up with ideas and making them happen, to holding the big picture when I get bogged down in detail, to supporting delivery and giving me vital feedback and advice. In terms of this book, Vicki sacrificed a huge amount of time, sleep and energy to look after our two young children so I could spend more time writing. My deepest love and appreciation goes to her, as well as to our wonderful boys Arthur and Barnaby, who brought me back to earth and attention when I began to get caught up in book-related concepts. You three are my mindfulness bells, and your chiming enriches my life more than I used to think possible...

References

Chapter 1

1. http://www.actionforhappiness.org/why-happiness

2. http://news.bbc.co.uk/1/hi/8230549.stm

3. Halliwell E. (2010), Mindfulness Report, Mental Health Foundation: London

4. http://ucsdnews.ucsd.edu/archive/newsrel/general/12-09Information.asp

5. http://www.dailymail.co.uk/health/article-1205669/Is-multi-tasking-bad-brain-Experts-reveal-hidden-perils-juggling-jobs.html

6. http://en.wikipedia.org/wiki/Continuous_partial_attention

7. http://www.psychologytoday.com/blog/the-mindful-self-express/201208/how-prevent-stress-shrinking-your-brain

8. http://www.buddhanet.net/pdf_file/powermindfulness.pdf

9. Halliwell E. (2010), Mindfulness Report, Mental Health Foundation: London

Mindfulness: the science
1. De Vibe et al. (2012) Mindfulness-based Stress Reduction (MBSR) for Improving Health, Quality of Life, and Social Functioning in Adults – *Campbell Collaboration Systematic Review* 2012

2. Khoury B. et al. (2013) Mindfulness-based Therapy: A Comprehensive Meta-analysis, *Clinical Psychology Review*, 33(6):763-71

3. Matousek et al. (2010) Cortisol as a Marker for Improvement in Mindfulness-Based Stress Reduction, *Complementary Therapies in Clinical Practice*, Feb 2010, pp13–19

4. Williams, Kuyken (2012) Mindfulness-based Cognitive Therapy: A Promising New Approach To Preventing Depressive Relapse, *British Journal of Psychiatry* 200: pp359–360

5. Zeidan et al. (2010) The Effects of Brief Mindfulness Meditation Training On Experimentally Induced Pain, *The Journal Of Pain*, March 2010, pp199–209

6. Rainer K. et al. (2013) Do Mindfulness-based Interventions Reduce Pain Intensity? A Critical Review of the Literature, *Pain Medicine*, 2013 Feb 14(2) pp230–42

7. Barrett et al. (2012) Meditation or Exercise for Preventing Acute Respiratory Infection: A Randomized Controlled Trial, *The Annals of Family Medicine*, July/August 2012 vol. 10 no. 4 pp337–346

8. Carlson (2012) Mindfulness-Based Interventions for Physical Conditions: A Narrative Review Evaluating Levels of Evidence, *ISRN Psychiatry*, vol. 2012

9. Chiesa et al. (2011) Does Mindfulness Training Improve Cognitive Abilities? A Systematic Review Of Neuropsychological Findings, *Clinical Psychology Review,* 31 pp449–464

10. Ostafin et al. (2012) Stepping Out of History: Mindfulness Improves Insight Problem Solving, *Consciousness and Cognition* vol 21, Issue 2, June 2012 pp1031–1036; Greenberg et al. (2012) Mind The Trap: Mindfulness Practice Reduces Cognitive Rigidity, PLOS One 7 (5)

11. Kirk et al. (2011) Interoception Drives Increased Rational Decision-Making In Meditators Playing The Ultimatum Game, *Frontiers in Neuroscience,* 2011 5: p49

12. Keng et al. (2011) Effects of Mindfulness on Psychological Health: A Review of Empirical Studies, *Clinical Psychology Review*, 31(6): pp1041–1056

13. Gross C.R. et al. (2011) Mindfulness-Based Stress Reduction vs. Pharmacotherapy for Primary Chronic Insomnia: A Pilot Randomized Controlled Clinical Trial, *Explore*, 7(2): 76–87, 2011.

14. Brown et al. (2007) Mindfulness: Theoretical Foundations and Evidence for its Salutary Effects, *Psychological Inquiry*, 2007, vol. 18, no. 4, 211–237

15. ibid

16. Barnes et al. (2007) The Role of Mindfulness in Romantic Relationship Satisfaction and Responses to Relationship Stress, *Journal of Marital and Family Therapy*, vol. 33, issue 4, pp482–500, October 2007

17. Keng et al. (2011) Effects of Mindfulness on Psychological Health: A Review of Empirical Studies, *Clinical Psychology Review*, 31(6): pp1041–1056

Mindfulness and neuroplasticity

1. Maguire et al. (2006) London Taxi Drivers and Bus Drivers: A Structural MRI and Neuropsychological Analysis, *Hippocampus* 16:pp1091–1101 (2006)

2. Gaser and Schlaug (2003) Brain Structures Differ between Musicians and Non-Musicians, *Journal of Neuroscience*, 23: pp9240–9245

3. http://lawsagna.typepad.com/lawsagna/2010/03/brain-awareness-week-15-amazing-examples-of-neuroplasticity-in-action-.html

4. ibid

5. Lazar (2005) Meditation Experience Is Associated With Increased Cortical Thickness, *Neuroreport*, vol. 18, no. 17, pp1893–1897; Davidson et al. (2003), Davidson, Kabat-Zinn (2003) Alterations In Brain And Immune System Function Produced By Mindfulness Meditation, *Psychosomatic Medicine*, 65: 564–70

6. Lutz et al. (2004) Long-term Meditators Self-induce High-amplitude Gamma Synchrony During Mental Practice, *PNAS* vol. 101 no. 46 pp16369–16373

7. Hölzel et al. (2011) Mindfulness Practice Leads To Increases In Regional Brain Gray Matter Density, *Psychiatry Research: Neuroimaging*, vol. 191, issue 1 pp36–43

Chapter 2

1. http://www.ted.com/talks/amy_cuddy_your_body_language_shapes_who_you_are.html

Chapter 3

1. http://en.wikipedia.org/wiki/Fight-or-flight_response

2. http://en.wikipedia.org/wiki/Implicit_memory

3. http://en.wikipedia.org/wiki/Negativity_bias

4. http://www.youtube.com/watch?v=Qb-gT6vDrmU

The science of mindful attention

1. Killingsworth M. and Gilbert D. (2010) A Wandering Mind Is An Unhappy Mind, *Science* vol. 330 p932

2. Keng et al. (2011) Effects of Mindfulness on Psychological Health: A Review of Empirical Studies, *Clinical Psychology Review*, 31(6): pp1041–1056

3. Maclean K. et al. (2010) Intensive Meditation Training Improves Perceptual Discrimination and Sustained Attention, *Psychological Science*, 21, pp829–839

4. Chiesa et al. (2010) Does Mindfulness Training Improve Cognitive Abilities? A Systematic Review of Neuropsychological Findings, *Clinical Psychology Review* 31, pp449–464

5. Mzarek et al. (2010) Mindfulness and Mind-Wandering: Finding Convergence Through Opposing Constructs, *Emotion*, vol. 2012, pp 442–448

6. Hölzel et al. (2012) How Does Mindfulness Meditation Work? Proposing Mechanisms Of Action From a Conceptual And Neural Perspective, *Perspectives On Psychological Science*, 6: 537, and Lazar et al. (2005) Meditation Experience Is Associated With Increased Cortical Thickness, *Neuroreport*, vol. 16, no. 17, pp1893–1897

7. Greenberg et al. (2012) 'Mind The Trap': Mindfulness Practice Reduces Cognitive Rigidity, PLOS One, (7) 5 e36206

Chapter 4

1. Thanks to Tara Brach for this exercise, see http://blog. tarabrach.com/2013/03/the-backward-step.html

2. Thanks to Shunryu Susuzi for this analogy, which is alluded to in Suzuki S. (1970) *Zen Mind, Beginner's Mind*, this edition (2011) Shambhala Publications, p18

3. Recounted in Merton T. (1965) *The Way Of Chuang Tzu, New Directions*, this edition (2010, p114)

Taking a breathing space

1. The three-step breathing space practice was developed as a part of the Mindfulness-Based Cognitive Therapy (MBCT) course, as described in Segal Z, Williams M, Teasdale J, (2002) *Mindfulness-Based Cognitive Therapy For Depression* (Guilford Press, 2012)

How awareness helps with low mood and anxiety

1. www.sciencedaily.com/releases/2013/04/130418154413.htm

2. www.bbc.co.uk/news/magazine-24444431

3. Mental Health Foundation (2007), *The Fundamental Facts: The Latest Facts and Figures on Mental Health* (London: Mental Health Foundation)

4. Keng et al. (2011) Effects of Mindfulness on Psychological Health: A Review of Empirical Studies, *Clinical Psychology Review* 31(6): pp1041–1056

5. Van Hugt (2012) The Effects of Mindfulness-based Cognitive Therapy on Affective Memory Recall Dynamics in Depression: A Mechanistic Model of Rumination, *Frontiers in Human Neurosciences*, 19;6:257

6. Greenberg et al. (2012) 'Mind The Trap': Mindfulness Practice Reduces Cognitive Rigidity, PLOS One 7(5): e36206. doi:10.1371/journal.pone.0036206

7. http://newsroom.ucla.edu/portal/ucla/that-giant-tarantula-is-terrifying-238055.aspx

Chapter 5

1. Thanks to Marsha Lucas for this story, which is also included in her book *Rewire Your Brain for Love: Creating Vibrant Relationships Using The Science of Mindfulness* (Hay House, 2012)

2. *Why Zebras Don't Get Ulcers* Robert M. Sapolsky (St Martin's Press, 2004)

3. http://greatergood.berkeley.edu/article/item/how_to_relieve_stress

4. http://www.accesstoinsight.org/tipitaka/sn/sn36/sn36.006.than.html

Stress and the science of mindfulness

1. Creswell et al. (2007) Neural Correlates of Dispositional Mindfulness During Affect Labeling, *Psychosomatic Medicine*, July/August 2007 vol. 69 no. 6 pp560–565

2. Brewer et al. (2011) Meditation Experience is Associated with Differences in Default Mode Network Activity and Connectivity, *PNAS* December 13, 2011 vol. 108 no. 50 pp20254–20259

3. http://www.dailymail.co.uk/health/article-2103095/Once-dismissed-pretentious-brain-scans-prove-Eastern-philosophies-effective-treating-mental-illness.html

4. Brewer et al. (2011) Meditation Experience is Associated with Differences in Default Mode Network Activity and Connectivity, *PNAS* December 13, 2011 vol. 108 no. 50 pp20254–20259

5. Matousek et al. (2010) Cortisol as a Marker for Improvement in Mindfulness-based Stress Reduction, *Complementary Therapies in Clinical Practice*, vol. 16, issue 1, February 2010, pp13–19

6. Rosenkranz et al. (2013) A Comparison of Mindfulness-based Stress Reduction and an Active Control in Modulation of Neurogenic Inflammation, *Brain, Behavior, and Immunity*, vol. 27, January 2013, pp174–184

7. Davidson et al. (2003) Alterations in Brain and Immune Function Produced by Mindfulness Meditation, *Psychosomatic Medicine*, July/August 2003 vol. 65 no. 4 564–570

8. Jacobs et al. (2011) Intensive Meditation Training, Immune Cell Telomerase Activity, and Psychological Mediators, *Psycho-*

neuroendocrinology, vol. 36, issue 5, June 2011, pp664–681

9. Melville et al. (2012) Fifteen Minutes of Chair-Based Yoga Postures or Guided Meditation Performed in the Office Can Elicit a Relaxation Response, *Evidence-Based Complementary and Alternative Medicine*, vol. 2012, article ID 501986, 9 pages, 2012. doi:10.1155/2012/501986

10. Keng et al. (2011) Effects of Mindfulness on Psychological Health: A Review of Empirical Studies, *Clinical Psychology Review*, vol. 31, issue 6, August 2011, pp 1041–1056

11. ibid

Chapter 6

1. Davidson et al. (2003) Alterations in Brain and Immune Function Produced by Mindfulness Meditation, *Psychosomatic Medicine*, July/August 2003 vol. 65 no. 4 564–570

2. Chodron P. (2010) *Taking The Leap: Freeing Ourselves From Old Habits And Fears*, Shambhala Publications, pp90–94

The science of turning towards

1. Zeidan F. et al. (2011) Brain Mechanisms Supporting the Modulation of Pain by Mindfulness Meditation, *The Journal of Neuroscience*, 6 April 2011, 31(14): pp 5540–5548

2. Creswell J.D. et al. (2007) Neural Correlates of Dispositional Mindfulness During Affect Labeling, *Psychosomatic Medicine*, Jul–Aug; 69(6): pp 560–5

The importance of body posture

1. Williams, Penman (2011) *Mindfulness: Finding Peace In A Frantic World*, (Piatkus) pp 92–3

2. http://www.theguardian.com/science/2012/jun/30/self-help-positive-thinking

3. ibid

Chapter 7

1. http://www.cs.princeton.edu/~rywang/berkeley/258/parable.html

2. http://www.dhammatalks.net/Books2/Bhikkhu_Buddhadasa_Keys_to_Natural_Truth.htm

3. Zimmerman J. et al. (2013) The Way We Refer To Ourselves Reflects How We Relate To Others: Associations Between First-person Pronoun Use and Interpersonal Problems, *Journal of Research in Personality*, vol. 47, issue 3, June 2013, pp218–225

4. Wei W.W. (1963) *Ask The Awakened: The Negative Way*, p7, edition published by Sentient (2002)

The science of interconnection

1. http://www.wildmind.org/blogs/on-practice/appreciation-is-contagious

http://blogs.psychcentral.com/mindfulness/2012/10/the-science-behind-why-everything-you-do-matters/

http://slooowdown.wordpress.com/2012/03/24/book-summary-of-connected-by-nicolas-christakis-james-fowler/

The research quoted comes from Christakis and Fowler *Connected: The Amazing Power of Social Networks and How They Shape Our Lives* (HarperPress, 2009)

2. http://userpage.fu-berlin.de/~health/support/schwarzer_rieckmann_in_weidner.pdf

3. http://www.psychologicalscience.org/index.php/news/releases/risk-factor-for-depression-can-be-contagious.html

4. http://bps-research-digest.blogspot.co.uk/2012/03/introducing-enclothed-cognition-how.html

5. Lee C. et al. (2011) Putting Like a Pro: The Role of Positive Contagion in Golf Performance and Perception PLOS ONE 6(10)

6. http://www.economist.com/news/science-and-technology/21565573-some-effects-smoking-may-be-passed-grandmother

The science of mindfulness and the self

1. http://www.psychologytoday.com/blog/your-brain-work/200910/the-neuroscience-mindfulness

2. ibid

3. Brewer J. et al. (2011) Meditation Experience is Associated with Differences in Default Mode Network Activity and Connectivity, *PNAS* vol. 108 no. 50, pp20254–20259

Chapter 8

1. Levy et al. (2012) The Effects of Mindfulness Meditation Training on Multitasking in a High-Stress Information Environment, *Graphics Interface* 2012

2. Flook et al. (2013) Mindfulness for Teachers: A Pilot Study to Assess Effects on Stress, Burnout, and Teaching Efficacy, *Mind, Brain and Education*, vol 7: 3 pp182–195 and Fortney et al. (2013) Abbreviated Mindfulness Intervention for Job Satisfaction, Quality of Life, and Compassion in Primary Care Clinicians: A Pilot Study, *Family Medicine*, vol 11:5 pp412–420

3. http://www.sciencedaily.com/releases/2013/09/130905202847.htm

http://link.springer.com/article/10.1007per cent2Fs12671-013-0202-1#page-1

http://www.medicalnewstoday.com/releases/262251.php

http://www.telegraph.co.uk/news/newstopics/howaboutthat/9989142/Meditating-helps-students-get-better-grades.html

http://www.ia.ucsb.edu/pa/display.aspx?pkey=2970

4. http://themindfulmanifesto.com/mindfulness-in-the-news.html

5. Ortner C.N.M. et al. (2007) Mindfulness Meditation And Reduced Emotional interference On A Cognitive Task, *Motivation and Emotion* (2007) 31: pp271–283. See also Mindful Emotion Regulation: An Integrative Review (2009) *Clinical Psychology Review*, pp560–572

6. Kuyken et al. (2010) How does Mindfulness-based Cognitive Therapy Work? *Behaviour Research and Therapy*, Nov;48(11): pp1105–127

7. https://webspace.utexas.edu/neffk/pubs/SCper cent20Germerper cent20Chapter.pdf

8. Geschwind N. et al. (2011) Mindfulness Training Increases Momentary Positive Emotions and Reward Experience in Adults Vulnerable to Depression: A Randomized Controlled Trial, *Journal of Consulting and Clinical Psychology*, 2011 Oct;79(5):pp618–28 New York: Guilford Press

9. Roberts-Wolfe D. et al. (2012) Mindfulness Training Alters Emotional Memory Recall Compared to Active Controls: Support for an Emotional Information Processing Model of Mindfulness, *Frontiers in Human Neuroscience*, 2012 Feb 13; 6:1

10. Brown et al. (2007) Mindfulness: Theoretical Foundations and Evidence for its Salutary Effects, *Psychological Inquiry*, vol. 18, issue 4, pp211–237

11. Gilbert, Waltz (2010) Mindfulness and Health Behaviours, *Mindfulness*, vol 1, 4, pp227–234

12. Brown, Kasser (2005) Are Psychological and Ecological Wellbeing Compatible? The Role of Values, Mindfulness and Lifestyle, *Social Indicators Research*, 74, pp349–368, and Brown et al. (2009) When What One Has Is Enough: Mindfulness, Financial Desire Discrepancy, And Subjective Wellbeing, *Journal of Research In Personality*, vol. 43, issue 5, pp727–636

13. Grepmai et al. (2007) Promoting Mindfulness in Psychotherapists in Training Influences the Treatment Results of their Patients: A Randomized, Double-Blind, Controlled Study, *Psychotherapy and Psychosomatics*, 2007;76(6):pp332–8

14. http://michael-chaskalson.blogspot.co.uk/2012/11/what-impact-does-leaders-mindfulness.html

15. http://www.pnas.org/content/107/12/5334.long

16. Dunne et al. (2008) Spending Money On Others Promotes Happiness, *Science*, vol. 319 no. 5870 pp.1687–1688

17. http://www.psychologytoday.com/blog/feeling-it/201211/the-best-kept-secret-happiness-compassion

18. http://www.wildmind.org/blogs/on-practice/smiling-your-way-to-kindness

19. Emmons, McCullough (2003) Counting Blessings Versus Burdens: An Experimental Investigation of Gratitude and

Subjective Wellbeing in Daily Life, *Journal of Personality and Social Psychology*, Vol. 84(2), pp377–389

20. http://www.theguardian.com/commentisfree/2014/jan/08/green-space-combat-depression-mental-health

21. http://plumvillage.org/mindfulness-practice/the-5-mindfulness-trainings/

22. http://www.neweconomics.org/projects/entry/five-ways-to-wellbeing

23. http://greatergood.berkeley.edu/article/item/how_positive_emotions_improve_our_health

24. Fredrickson et al. (2008) Positive Emotions, Induced Through Loving-Kindness Meditation, Build Consequential Personal Resources, *Journal of Personal and Social Psychology*, 95(5): pp1045–1062

25. Weng et al. (2013) Compassion Training Alters Altruism and Neural Responses to Suffering, *Psychological Science*, May 21, 2013 and Condon et al. (2013) Meditation Increases Compassionate Responses to Suffering, *Psychological Science*, October 2013 vol. 24 no.10 pp2125–2127

26. Pace et al. (2009) Effect of Compassion Meditation on Neuroendocrine, Innate Immune and Behavioral Responses to Psychosocial Stress, *Psychoneuroendocrinology* 34(1): pp87–98

The three-step breathing space, with action step

1. http://greatergood.berkeley.edu/article/item/taking_in_the_good

Index

ABOUT THE AUTHOR

Vicki Halliwell

Ed Halliwell is a UK-based mindfulness teacher and writer. He leads courses and retreats in London, Sussex and Surrey, working with a wide range of groups and organizations. Ed is the co-author of *The Mindful Manifesto: How Doing Less And Noticing More Can Help Us Thrive In A Stressed-Out World* and author of *Into the Heart of Mindfulness*. He appears regularly in the media and at conferences, festivals and events, and is a teacher on the Mental Health Foundation's 'Be Mindful' online course, as well as an associate of the Oxford Mindfulness Centre. He is also a trustee of The Mindfulness Initiative, which is working with Parliamentarians to bring mindfulness into public policy. He blogs for mindful.org.

www.edhalliwell.com